THE GODS OF QUALITY
STRIKE BACK

Also by Paul Uduk

BRIDGES TO THE CUSTOMER'S HEART

THE GODS OF

QUALITY

STRIKE BACK

**The Rise and Near *Fall* of an Iconic Bank,
How it Flunked the Ultimate Test
and Paid a Humiliating Price:
The Unauthorised Story
and Other Lessons on
Excellence**

Paul Uduk

Order this book online at www.trafford.com
or email orders@trafford.com

Most Trafford titles are also available at major online book retailers.

Printed in the United States of America.

ISBN: 978-1-4269-7224-9 (sc)
ISBN: 978-1-4269-7225-6 (e)

Trafford rev. 07/29/2011

 www.trafford.com

North America & International
toll-free: 1 888 232 4444 (USA & Canada)
phone: 250 383 6864 ♦ fax: 812 355 4082

Dedication

This book is dedicated to

…Mallam Sanusi Lamido Sanusi

Governor, Central Bank of Nigeria,

…for uncommom courage.

Acknowledgements

Writing is a lonely enterprise. However, lurking below the surface of that loneliness always are the encouraging voices of countless people cheering you on to the finishing line. The most difficult decision then is deciding who to leave out when writing an acknowledgement. Should you acknowledge all that gave you thumbs up or only the most strident supporters? My answer, all deserve a mention. But at this instance, I wish to acknowledge just one person: my former English teacher at Holy Family College, Oku Abak, Akwa Ibom State. To us he was 'Mbomm'. Yes, 'Mbomm' was his knickname.

Mbomm was the epitome of dedication, care, and passion. He never left a single exercise in the recommended English text book untouched. He never raised a voice on any student. His ability to motivate was second to none. After our WAEC English examination paper I and about six of my co-conspirators met him on the corridor and he asked, "how was it"?, directing the question to no one in particular. Since no one spoke, I mumbled something to the effect that the paper was too *hard*. He looked me square at the face, smiled, and boomed, "if you don't have A1, you have yourself to blame", and with that he strutted away, as happy as ever. Mbomm personified Quality. Yes, Quality with capital Q! He died a few years ago before I had the opportunity to tell him what a great teacher he was. Mbomm did his bit so all errors you may find here, both grammatical and conceptual, are entirely mine.

CONTENTS

Prologue

The list of once great companies that have fallen by the way side or have been taken over by rivals for a pittance for failing the *Quality Test* reads like Forbes *Who Is Who?* They include Borders, Arthur Anderson, Enron, WorldCom, Global Crossings, Lehman Brothers, Merrill Lynch, Long Term Capital, Northern Rock, to mention but a few. The unmistakable message is: the *Gods of Quality* are no respecter of persons and institutions and will strike back once you turn your back on customers and continue to desecrate the hallowed chambers of excellence with impunity.

The immediate impetus to this book is the sad state of Union Bank of Nigeria Plc., once one of the triumphirate that constitututed the BIG THREE in Nigeria's banking firmament, the others being First Bank of Nigeria Plc. and the United Bank for Africa Plc. In a systematic, audacious and professionally coordinated move, the Central Bank of Nigeria led by Mallam Sanusi Lamido Sanusi on August 14, 2009 seized the assets of five 'gravely sick' banks in the country, and sacked their CEOs, including those of Union Bank of Nigeria Plc., Intercontinental Bank Plc., Oceanic International Bank Plc., Finbank Plc., and Afribank Nigeria Plc., signifying the end of an era for the Nigerian banking industry, and sadly so for the 92 year old iconic bank. Union Bank indeed once had a glorious past, but had been left in the dust by its arch rivals,

First Bank and UBA, and its fate, and those of its over 8,000 employees now hang in the balance, with investors willing to come to its rescue from the ignominy of liquidation no where in sight as at the time of publication. Will Union be allowed to die? Can a miracle save the Stallion? The fate of Union is yet another pointed reminder that no organization can be a rock of Gibraltar, unchanging, deaf, dumb and internally focused and hope to survive in this new brave dispensation where the world is *flat*. As this book was being rushed to bed, Union Bank's management led by the CBN appointed caretaker MD, Mrs. Funke Osibodu was in a running battle with NLC (Nigeria Labour Congress) for the soul of UNION, for proscribing the local ASSBIFI (Association of Senior Staff of Banks, Insurance and Other Financial Institutions) wing of Union Bank. Death threats have been issued against the ''iron lady'', court order restraining NLC from picketing the bank have been issued, and violated, and both side have dug in for what NLC's has called *total war*. The air has been so foul, Union Bank's management had to escape to volatile Maiduguri in Nigeria's extreme North East for a hurried Annual General Meeting in January 2011, unlike in the past where prestigious Abuja would have been the AGM's venue.

As part of an MBA project at Ahmadu Bello University, Zaria, circa 1995, we had sufficient evidence to conclude that there was a distinct possibility of the so called new generation banks overtaking the BIG THREE if they did not change their bad old ways and change pretty fast. Frustration with the BIG THREE had reached a crescendo in the late eighties culminating in the entry into the industry of the *new generation* banks led by Zenith (1987), GTB (1990) and Diamond (1991). With their boutique operations at the time, business automation, and nimble staff, the new generation banks were turning banking on its head, and were nibbling at the deposit foundations of the old generation banks.

Service delivery was so appalling in the old generation banks, especially in the BIG THREE, that the then New Nigeria Bank had at the time an advertisement with a bank customer arriving at his bank with a sleeping mat, with the branch manager exclaiming, "oh you don't need a mattress here", the unmistakable message being that you won't sleep in our bank if you come to do business with us, an indirect reference to the snail speed of operations in the then BIG THREE. To lend my voice to the frustration we all felt, I had in an article **Towards Improved Banking Services** published in the now rested The Democrat March 26, 1992, cried out, saying *"Service in majority of the banks is invariably sloppy, one is left to wonder if they are in competition to determine which among them is the most sloppy."*

The fate of Union Bank did not come as a total surprise but what surprised keen industry observers and business students alike was why the bank stubbornly refused to change, despite warnings and the unmistakable signs that the competitive landscape had irreversibly changed. On June 5, 2005 at a CIBN (Chartered Institute of Bankers of Nigeria) organised Annual Bankers Lecture at Sheraton Hotel, Ikeja, where Mr.

G. A. T. Oboh, the then Group Managing Director of Union Bank presented a lead paper, with protocols duly observed, I had asked Mr. Oboh during the question and answer session why the BIG THREE refused to show leadership and were only contented to play *catch up* with the *new generation* banks. Mr. Oboh dismissed my question, and amid a thunderous applause from Union Bank employees that constituted 50 per cent of the audience, said, *"young man, where are you from, I'm sure before you were born there was a branch of Union Bank in your village, so what are you talking about."* I was dumbfounded! Mr. Oboh had totally missed the strategic thrust of my question, and many of the Union Bank employees in the audience queried my temerity for asking their Managing Director such a pedantic question. The employees too had missed the train! Mr. Femi Pedro, the then Chief Executive Officer of the then Comet Bank, the precursor to FinBank Plc., who later became the Deputy Governor of Lagos State, even counselled me. He said, *"you should have used more tact."* In short, Mr. Pedro was reminding me the sad reality that in Nigeria you don't question *authority.* I was alone that day.

The aim of my question was to stimulate debate, to challenge the BIG THREE to show more leadership in dictating the pace of change and development in the financial services sector rather than play catch-up. I sought to point out that the BIG THREE needed to show leadership in key areas such as automation of processes, attitude to the customer, being more welcoming, being more strategic, you name it. In all these areas, the BIG THREE had at the time lagged behind the *new generation* banks. As Tom Peters said in one of his recent daily quotes, *"EXCELLENCE is the next meeting. Or it is nothing at all. EXCELLENCE is about now, not some mythical future state."* Tom went on to say, again recently in his daily quote, *"One satisfied customer telling a friend, an acquaintance, a cousin, a bus driver, a total stranger how happy he is with your service is worth its weight in gold (or five times its weight in advertising dollars)."* We pray that for Union Bank these lessons have not come too late!

How did we come to the conclusion that the BIG THREE needed to do something fast to avert disaster? We modelled our project after Fortune's annual survey for the most admired companies. Annually Fortune magazine carries out a survey that asks 8,000 senior executives, outside directors, and financial analysts to rate companies in their industries on eight attributes using a scale of 0 (poor) to 10 (excellent). Though the attributes have been changed slightly, at the time of our study they were as follows:

- Quality of Management
- Quality of Products or Services
- Innovativeness
- Long-term Investment Value
- Financial Soundness
- Ability to Attract, Develop and Keep Talented People
- Responsibility to the Community and the Environment
- Wise Use of Corporate Assets

In their 1992/93 survey, the most admired company was Merck and Company, with an average score of 8.74. The least admired was Wang Laboratories with an average score of 1.99. Fortune's 1993/94 survey, when our project started, had Rubbermaid as the most admired company. The most admired company in 1994/95 when our project ended was GE. In recent years Apple has been the most admired company, claiming the top spot for three years in a row, 2008, 2009, and 2010.

The project which metamorphosed into this book was inspired by this annual Fortune magazine survey. We were interested to know the *Quality of Customer Service* in the Nigerian Banking industry, an attribute identical to *Quality of Products and Services* listed number two in the Fortune's list. This attribute was selected because the candidate had been a "Quality" enthusiast ever since being exposed in the early nineties to the "Quality Management" concept, now used broadly interchangably with *Excellence*.

The quality management concept is now being used in various contexts in the financial services sector. The approach involves a disciplined search for answers to four basic questions[1]:
  1. Who are the customers?
  2. What do they want?
  3. How is the product or service best delivered?
  4. What is the best path to continuous improvement?

From available evidence, two commercial banks in Nigeria, Crystal Bank of Africa Ltd. (which went comatose and later resurrected and changed its name to Standard Trust Bank, and eventually took over UBA), and Guaranty Trust Bank Ltd., had at inception adopted the **"Quality Management"** philosophy in the management of their banks and have been, especially Guaranty Trust Bank, very successful with sustainable profits since inception in 1990. Guaranty Trust Bank (GTBank) is so successful that it's today quoted on both the Nigerian Stock Exchange (NSE) and the London Stock Exchange (LSE), and recently raised $350mm from the international capital market via bond issuance, the first of its kind in the annals of Nigerian banking . However, at the time of our project the new generation banks served niche markets quite distinct from the mass market the BIG THREE we investigated served.

We decided to use the BIG THREE as our case study since they had, and still have, the largest branch networks, deposit bases, and employ the largest number of staff. In the 90s when Nigerians talked about banks, they had First Bank, Union Bank and UBA in mind. When systemic distress hit the banking industry around 1993 following 'June 12' (see footnotes at the end of this section for the meaning of 'June 12'), and its aftermath, all the deposit flights or flight to quality from the remaining 117 banks at the time went to the BIG THREE. Using them as case study was therefore justified since they had the greatest capacity to bring about any significant change in the system overall. Being the oldest surviving banks in the country (First Bank: 1894, Union: 1917, UBA: 1949) they had and somehow still have the historically determined mandate to bring about positive changes in the industry.

The study rated the BIG THREE on fourteen *performance* attributes, determinants of service quality, based on the *importance* customers attach to these attributes. The attibutes were originally developed by Berry et al and have been widely accepted in the literature[2]. Based on the outcome, we drew deductions and made recommendations, and pointed the way forward for the BIG THREE. What we found is what you are about to read.

Of the three, only First Bank did something about our findings. I had met Dr. Alli Balogun, then part of First Bank's Human Resources Management team, at a seminar, and had shared our alarming findings with him and he immediately invited me to his office for more. That day after I told Dr. Balogun all I needed to, I concluded with the saying by Deming *"Quality is what the customer says it is."* With that we shook hands and he said, we will get back to you. I never heard from him again. But FBN did something about our findings, culminating in their **Century Two Project.**

I made contact with UBA through Dr. Boniface Chizie, then of UBA's Strategic Planning Department, who then put me through to Dr. (Mrs) Chukwunekwue, the then Head of Human Resources Management Department. I spent two hours waiting to see her, and when I was finally ushered in to meet with her, she didn't pay much attention to what I was trying to say. She politely told me she was a little bit busy and needed to consult with others and would get back to me. At the back of her mind, she thought I came to look for a job. In all, that was the last I heard from her until Dr. Hakeem Osagie took over the bank. As for Union Bank, all attempts to see any person of status failed. I visited their Regional Office at Bank Road, Kaduna, uncountable number of times and the best they did was to direct me to Stallion House, at Marina, Lagos, their 29 story head office, and symbol of what Union Bank thought was their greatness. I made it to Stallion House, but with all my persistence, oratory and, cajolling I only managed to pass the ground floor reception personnel, manned by securitymen in light brown uniforms, that wispered to me 'good luck' as they allowed me to proceed to the sixth floor of their 29 story edifice. I was not lucky! The sixth floor was where the General Managers were sequestrated, so to say. The security men on the sixth floor said I needed a special pass and an appointment to go pass them. My persistence failed. My oratory evaporated. My cajolling came to a grinding halt and the security personnel stared at me, triumphantly. One GM passed by and never bothered to ask who I was and what my mission was. I understood even staff as high as Assistant General Managers needed to complete *visitors' form* before being allowed to the sixth floor.

All my attempts to meet with the managing directors of the BIG THREE failed. The failure goes to show how rigid our organizations are. In most countries, just a phone call can open the door to meet with anybody. NOT SO IN NIGERIA.

Nigerian organizations need to change, be more transparent, and the high and mighty must make themselves more accessible to the people they serve. Some CEOs, including the founders of the mega churches, go in convoys and use bullet proof amored vehicles. With fierce looking bouncers, you dare not go near them. Beware, you are there to serve if you call yourself a leader. A leader is a servant, a steward and a shephered. A leader does not lord it over the people. A leader *'puts a dent in the universe'* as Steve Jobs, Apple co-founder dreamt and continues to dream. According to Marcus Buckingham, "Leaders are fascinated by the future. You are a leader if, and only if, you are restless for change, impatient for progress, and deeply dissatisfied with the status quo." "As a leader" he explains, "you are never satisfied with the present, because in your head you can see a better future, and the friction between 'what is' and 'what could be' burns you, stirs you up, propels you forward. This is leadership."[3] According to Marcus Buckingham, "Great leaders rally people to a better future."

Nigerian organizations must change if they are to survive and thrive. Change don't happen, it must start with YOU! Tom Peters once said *"People and organizations, if they do change, change themselves. At best, we consultants can hold their individual/collective hands, and whisper words of wisdom and encouragement, which will never be heard until the exact accidental moment when they are ready to hear them for their own sweet reasons!"[4]* Did Union Bank miss its *exact accidental moment*? What could they have done differently? What lessons can you draw as you navigate your career, lead your company, or community? What lessons can organizations, big and small, draw to avert disaster in this new brave flat world, where things must be done with speed and agility, beauty and passion, panache and elegance. Let's go there. To our reason why, we scurry.

Footnote: June 12 has to do with the June 12, 1993 polls in Nigeria. Late Bashorun Moshood Kashimowo Olawole Abiola (MKO) of the Social Democratic Party swept the polls and the Military junta under General Ibrahim Badamasi Babangida annulled the elections throwing the country into a near war situation. General Babangida later stepped aside, and an Interim Government under Mr. Ernest Shonekan was inaugurated and promptly declared illegal by a High Court, followed by General Sanni Abacha's palace coup six months later. Pro-Democracy movement led by Nobel Laurate, Professor Wole Soyinka, Prof. Pat Utomi, Asiwaju (Senator) Bola Tinubu, the late Gani Fawihinmi SAN, late Mrs. Kudirat Abiola, late Dr. Abraham Adesanya, to mention but the arrow head, called on the military to respect the sanctity of the people's mandate to Abiola and insisted on *"June 12."* June 12 lingered until May 27, 1999 when another general election brought General Olusegun Obasanjo to power. June 12 1993 then is the precursor to Democracy in Nigeria, a date never to be forgotten.

Chapter One

WHAT DO BANKS REALLY DO?

*"We are what we repeatedly do. Excellence, then is not
an act, but a habit."*

ARISTOTLE

Traditionally banks are organisations engaged in financial
intermediation business. In very simple terms, banks borrow
money from those that have some to spare and lend to those
in need and get compensated for the service. Professor
David Llewellyn of Loughborough University Banking Centre
in an article in Banking World of January 1995 entitled
The Changing Nature of Banking described a financial
intermediary as *"an institution which accepts deposits with
one set of characteristics and makes loans or acquires assets
with a different set".*[1]

Banks in Nigeria have been faithfully performing this traditional
function for over 116 years since the first bank was established
in 1894. That bank was British Bank of West Africa, now First
Bank of Nigeria Plc. From their humble beginnings in 1894,
banks in Nigeria by 1992 totalled 120. The phenomenal
growth in bank numbers between the period 1985 and 1994
had been traced to the Structural Adjustment Programme of

the General Babangida administration with its emphasis on deregulation and competition.

The objective of deregulation is the creation of a level playing field for the participants of the market place. In a deregulated, competitive economy, government attempts to create a level playing field by removing from the field of play as many obstacles as possible, leaving the ingenuity and the competitive urges of individual management teams to resolve matters. By doing so competition is encouraged, with the customer being the ultimate beneficiary.

Heightened competition means pressure on banks will intensify. Writing in **Banking World** of January 1995 Prof. Llewellyn highlighted the formidable challenges banks around the world were already facing. He emphasised that banks were losing some of their past monopolies and comparative advantages which had underpinned their position in the financial system. Prof. Llewellyn concluded with the words *''There is now little that banks do that could not be done either by the capital markets, by non-banking financial institutions, or by non-financial banking institutions. Banks are no longer the exclusive suppliers of banking services.''*[2]

Competition has a powerful impact on all industries. However, Prof. David Llewellyn pointed out that competition was *"working asymmetrically"* in the financial industry. Because of developments in technology and general erosion of entry barriers into banking, Prof. Llewellyn emphasised that *"it was easier for non-bank financial institutions and non-financial banking institutions to diversify into banking than it was for banks to diversify out of financial services".[3]* Accordingly, quality of products and services will emerge as the most important differentiating factor among banks. The weak in this regard will die. That is why within a few short years of existence, Diamond Bank, GT Bank, Zenith Bank had earned reputation as the banks of choice for quality service in Nigeria and continue to power on. Today, Zenith and GTB have supplanted Union Bank and are ranked as Nigeria's first tier banks along with First bank and UBA, while Diamond has fallen to the second tier.

Quality service refers to how a product or service is packaged and how it is delivered. The entire focus of the quality service paradigm is customer satisfaction. For the service provider it is not enough to say we stand for this or we stand for that. What the institution stands for must be translated into concrete action by the way it relates to its customers.

Banks will need to be more efficient and innovative to withstand competition. The quality management concept is now being used in various contexts in the financial services sector. The concept and its related practices is generally refered to as **TOTAL QUALITY MANAGEMENT (TQM)** or its variations, **TOTAL QUALITY SERVICE (TQS)** or **TOTAL CUSTOMER SERVICE.** As we earlier pointed out, TQM involves a disciplined search for answers to four related questions:

1. Who are the customers?
2. What do they want?

3. How is the product or service best delivered?

4. What is the best path to continuous improvement?[4]

Kevin Gavaghan, the then Marketing Director (UK Banking) of Midland Bank, which once ranked as UK's third largest bank, emphasised in an article, **Banks Go Marketing**, published in Banking World of March 1990 that there was a major opportunity available to banks that moved to differentiate themselves from competition by establishing a reputation for providing a tangible high quality service for customers. Successful banks, according to Gavaghan, *"will be those that respond to the paradigm of changing and increasing customer expectation in the best intergarted, most stable and responsive way, while maintaing profitability at a level acceptable to the owners of the business."* [5]

Late Brain Pitman, the then Chief Executive Officer (CEO) of Lloyds Bank Plc., in an interview in Banking World of April 1988 emphasised that *"it is a myth that the biggest is the best. It is much more difficult to be the best than to be the biggest. And the best I believe is the strongest, and most profitable. Among the banks, the best is the one with the highest reputation for serving customers and having the highest quality staff."* [6]

Nigeria has always been known for a vibrant banking industry, with a proliferation of banks, rising in numbers from 28 in 1984 to 120 in 1992. By the third quarter of 1993 the industry as a whole experienced systemic distress characterised by capital inadequacy, illiquidity and loses. The Central Bank of Nigeria responded to these problems by liquidating the terminally sick banks and taking over the moribund ones with a view to saving those that could be saved and liquidating eventually those that it could not. By September 1995 five banks had been liquidated and 22 others had been taken over and put under the direct management of the CBN and Nigerian Deposit Insurance Corporation (NDIC). Amongst the liquidated banks was the once high flying Alpha Merchant Bank Plc.

The common denominator underpinning all banks as they grew in numbers was poor service. Banks were totally unresponsive to customers needs. In the majority of the banks customers had to wait long hours to encash their cheques, most banks never bothered to send account statements to customers. Banks staff were unfriendly and lacking in courtesy, and most did not know why they were employed. These short comings created room for the emergence of the new generation banks that employed only graduates. The likes of Diamond Bank started from day one with full automation, offering on-line real-time services using what it called the DIBS (Diamond Integrated Banking Services) advantage, with MicroBanker developed by the then Citibank (now Citigroup) as the IT platform.

The BIG THREE never even noticed the challenge the new generation banks posed. We however anticipated the demise of the BIG THREE and in a series of articles pointedly said so. In an article, **The Importance of Quality In Banking**, the author wrote *"It is desperately important banks realised that they are in the service industry and must give excellent service - good or average service is not enough."*[7] We somewhat predicted the emergence of the new generation banks as the new power houses when in the same article we advised the new generation banks to learn from the mistakes of their forebears, saying "*The new generation banks are uniquely placed to tap to the fullest the benefits of deregulation. They are not shackled by bad debts and from the benefit of handsight, can foreswear never to repeat the mistakes of their big flabby peers – arrogance, unapproachability, unfriendliness.*"[8]

The signs were ominous so we dug deep to investigate and confirm our hunches, praying we would be proven wrong. This project looked at the **IMPORTANCE** bank customers attached to fourteen attributes we defined as **DETERMINANTS OF SERVICE QUALITY** (or testers of quality) and how the BIG THREE rated in their **PERFORMANCE** in these service attributes. Arising from the findings, we drew inferences on what the attitudes of the BIG THREE were as regards providing *Quality Service* to their teeming customers. As at the time of the project, the BIG THREE controlled over 70% of the deposit and asset bases of the banking industry, and accounted for 33% of the branch network (744 out of 2259). In embarking on this journey we solicited the cooperation of the CBN and NDIC to make available sensitive data in their custody but received no response so we used data available in the public domain and justified our resolve as follows:

1. **Quality Management** though extensively practised in Japan, the US and Western Europe, is new in Nigeria.

It's study therefore will increase the level of awareness of the subject within the country.

2. Quality is widely regarded as a strategic weapon. Adoption of **Quality Management** practices will mean that Nigerian banks will be regarded as reliable partners to do business with by the international banking community

3. The link between quality and profitability has been well established by other studies such as the **Profit Impact of Market Strategies** (PIMS) studies in the US. Widescale adoption of **Total Quality Management** practices in the banking industry in Nigeria could therefore lead to rapid recovery of the industry currently plagued by mismanagement.

4. The goal of quality management is to achieve continuous improvement in customer satisfaction. Pursuit of customer satisfaction by banks would restore confidence in the banking industry which will lead to increased business and higher savings mobilisation. The combined effects of the above should lead to rapid growth of the banking industry and thus stimulate the recovery of the economy as a whole.

To explore this interesting subject further let's first look at the the birth of Quality, the conceptual framework, standards, awards, prizes, misconconceptions and what the Quality Gurus and pioneers have to say.

Chapter Two

QUALITY: MASTERING THE CONCEPTUAL
FRAMEWORK - LESSONS FROM THE QUALITY GURUS

*"There are only two qualities in the world, efficiency
and inefficiency; and only two sorts of people,
the efficient and the inefficient."*

GEORGE BERNARD SHAW

Peter Drucker was once asked what he thought about gurus, and he said that the word charlatan was too difficult to pronounce so people coined the word guru. Peter Drucker, who Tom Peters described as the "creator and inventor of modern management", was in effect saying that there are no gurus because what may be right or correct today may become totally wrong or irrelevant tomorrow. However, for the purposes of this book, we will call the pioneering fathers quality gurus.

According to Stebbing, the word quality in the ordinary meaning of the word implies "subjective judgment". Quality, like beauty, is in the eyes of the beholder. What is considered by one person to be of good quality could be considered by another to be of poor quality and vice versa. In the context of Total

Quality Assurance or Total Quality Management, however, quality has a precise meaning. It is defined as:

"The totality of features and characteristics of a product or service that bears on its ability to satisfy stated or implied needs." (ISO 8402-1986: Quality Vocabulary). [1]

In addition to the above standard definition given by the International Organization for Standardization (ISO) based in Geneva, many writers and the quality gurus have given their own definitions of quality. For instance Joseph Juran defined quality as *"fitness for purpose of use".*[2] While Phillip Crosby said *"quality means conformance".*[3] In the film, Journey to Excellence, which has done a lot to stimulate interest of Nigerians towards quality, Mike Robson defined quality as *"meeting the agreed requirements of the customer, now and in the future".*[4] Adedeji Badiru and Babatunde Ayeni in the book **Practitioner's Guide to Quality and Process Improvement** gave the following systems-oriented definition of quality: *"Quality refers to an equilibrium level of functionality possessed by a product or service based on the producer's capability and customer needs."*[5]

The producer's capability, according to Badiru and Ayeni, is defined *"by the aggregate capabilities of the people, machine, other production facilities available to the producer".*[6] The customer's needs, they stated, are defined *"by a combination of what the customer wants and what the customer needs, and what the customer favors. Each component of the producer's capability and the customer's need may be viewed as a subsystem of the overall quality management system."[7]*

Dr. Armand V. Feigenbaum is the best known advocate of a total system approach to quality. A Total Quality System is defined as *"the agreed companywide and plantwide operating work structure, documented in effective, integrated, technical and managerial procedures, for guiding the coordinated actions of the people, the machines and the information of the company and plant in the best most practical ways to assure customer quality satisfaction and economical cost of quality."[8]*

According to Bendell, *''Quality is in essence a way of managing the organization and has now become an essential element of modern management."[9]*

While many definitions have been proposed, most can be summarised by one of the following two statements:

1. Conformance to specification - Quality is defined by the relative absence of defects.
2. Meeting customer requirement - Quality is measured by the degree of customer satisfaction with a product's (service's) characteristics and features.[10]

Buzzell and Gale (1987) distinguished between relative *"perceived"* quality and *"conformance"* quality, which is the traditional way quality is normally thought of. Relative perceived quality, as the authors pointed out, is not identical to "conformance" quality. Relative perceived quality is different and demands an entirely new perspective - one that calls for viewing quality externally, from the customer's perspective, rather than internally, from quality assurance point of view.[11] Adherence to "conformance" quality and relative perceived quality is the essence and at the heart of the Total Quality Movement.

BACKGROUND TO THE QUALITY MOVEMENT, STANDARD, AWARD AND PRIZES

BACKGROUND TO THE QUALITY MOVEMENT

The Quality Guru, Feigenbaum, as quoted by Bendell, has identified quality as *"the single most important force in organizations success and growth."*[12] According to Badiru and Ayeni, *"the quality of products and services will be one common basis for trade communication in the global village. Companies and countries must recognize the trend and refocus their efforts."*[13] According to Laura A. Liswood, the then Chairman of Westinghouse Electric, John C. Marous, in 1990, told a **"Quest for Excellence"** Conference in Washington D.C. that *"total quality is the absolute answer to all our problems, professionally and personally, in this country".*[14]

So how and where did the quality movement all begin? Let us answer that question with another question. Which country makes the best cars, motorcycles, cameras, television sets, videos, watches, to mention a few. The answer is Japan . It is now generally known that the quality movement started in Japan and this helped them to achieve world economic dominance within a relatively short period of 40 years, from the end of the Second World War in 1945.[15] According to Badiru and Ayeni, the emergence of Japan as an economic leader has had a profound effect on the quality revolution.[16]

Dr. William Edward Deming laid the foundation for the quality movement that started in Japan . The Japanese enthusiastically adopted and methodically implemented Deming's philosophies to improve the quality of their products and services. The Japanese approach to quality is simple, straight forward and effective. It is the simplicity of the approach that makes it understandable and workable in any organization. In a Japanese production environment, according to Badiru and Ayeni, quality is viewed as *"bottom-up, top-down and lateral integration of functions."* [17]

According to Professor Ishikawa, in Japan *"quality refers not only to quality of product but also of after-sales service, quality of management, the company itself and the human being."*[18] The drive and the motivation for quality improvement is one of Japan's major export to the rest of the world. In 1961 Juran, one of the world's quality gurus, pointed out that the Japanese attention to quality improvement would be the impetus that would take them to the top of the world market. The key to the success of Japan in the world market, according to Badiru and Ayeni, lies in the *"multilateral approach to quality management."* The approach covers the following elements:

- Avenues for identifying, analyzing and correcting mistakes are put in place.
- Significant emphasis is placed on training.
- Each employee is given the basic tools needed for quality improvement efforts.
- Attitude of pride in workmanship is encouraged throughout the organization.

- Each employee is empowered to preside over the quality issues affecting her job.
- Each employee exhibits a sense of responsibility for the products and services she generates.[19]

Japan's success has established the yardstick by which all quality improvement measures will be measured throughout the world. Japanese quality improvement and management improvement models are now being widely adopted all over the world. Most of the basic tools that the Japanese use to study and improve quality originated from western organizations. In the 1970s, western companies began to recognize and accept the fact that Japanese success in the world marketplace was as a resulf of the high quality of products offered by Japan. Western companies that originally ignored Deming's philosophies then began searching to find out how Japan turned the philosophy into pragmatic production approaches. Awareness of the Japanese approach to quality led American industry to begin to focus on the quality management and statistical techniques which were disseminated through numerous publications. [20]

QUALITY STANDARDS

The Japanese initiated the quality revolution in the 1950s and the Americans and Western Europe joined the movement in the 1970s. Today the quality movement is gathering momentum worldwide as companies and countries jostle for competitive advantage. The striving for better quality has led to the need for unified international quality standards. The International Organization for Standardization (ISO) in Geneva, Switzerland, is the organization charged with developing quality standards internationally. The agency as at the time of our study was made up of the national standard bodies of 91 countries, however, today that number has increased to 160. At the time the agency prepared the quality standard known as ISO 9000. The standards were first published in 1987. They were developed to help companies effectively document the quality system elements required to maintain an efficient quality system. They are not specific to any industry, product or service. ISO 9000 is a set of individual but related international standards on quality management and quality assurance. The five individual standards that make up the ISO 9000 series are:

ISO 9000 – This is the roadmap that provides guidelines for selecting and using ISO 9001, ISO 9002, ISO 9003 and ISO 9004. A supplementary publication, ISO 8402, provides quality related definitions. ISO 9000 is entitled Quality Management and Quality Assurance Standards: Guidelines for use.

ISO 9001 – This standard presents a comprehensive model for quality assurance for design, manufacturing, installation and servicing systems.

ISO 9002 – This present a model for quality assurance in production and installation.

ISO 9003 – This presents a model of quality assurance in final inspection and test.

ISO 9004 – This provides guidelines to users in the process of developing in house quality systems.

The ISO 9000 series standards define the minimum requirements a supplier must meet to assure its customers that they are receiving high quality products. Companies that are certified and registered as meeting ISO standards will be perceived as viable suppliers to their customers. This has had a major impact on companies around the world. Through ISO 9000 standard, businesses can now be evaluated consistently and uniformly.[21]

The ISO 9000 series has been adopted in the U.S by the American National Standards Institute (ANSI) and the American Society for Quality Control (ASQC) as ANSI/ASQC Q90 standards. The European equivalent of ISO 9000 is the EN 29000 series, while the British equivalent is the BS 5750 series. Nigeria at the time of our study had not formally adopted the ISO 9000 standards and products were certified to the Nigerian Industrial Standard   (NIS) Product Quality Mark administered by the Standard Organization of Nigeria (SON). Products that maintain their quality for up to 5, and 10 years, are respectively awarded "Silver" and "Gold" versions of the NIS mark. On its website visited on February 17, 2011, the International Organisation for Standardisation (ISO) stated *"ISO has developed over 18,500 International Standards on a variety of subjects and some 1,100 new ISO standards are published every year."*

QUALITY AWARDS AND PRIZES

To create awareness, reduce resistance and challenge organizations to aim at higher quality, countries and International Agencies and Organizations institute prizes for companies and individuals as a means of recognition. In Japan , the Deming prize was established in 1951 to commemorate the friendship and achievements of Dr. W. Edward Deming. It consists of two different awards the Deming Prize and the Prize for Application, which are awarded to individuals or companies after examination by the Deming Prize Committee. This committee is not governmental. The award is considered to be the most distinguished Quality Control Award and there are many companies which make the prize their first goal in their efforts for the promotion of quality control (QC). According to Bendell, the Prizes play a major role in the promotion of Quality Control (QC), Statistical Quality Control (SQC) and Companywide Quality Control (CWQC) in Japan.[22]

In the US , the Malcolm Baldrige National Quality Award (MBNQA) is the most coveted Prize. The award was established by Congress and was signed into law by President Ronald Reagan on August 20, 1987 as the Malcolm Baldrige National Quality Improvement Act. The award was set up by the US Department of Commerce in memory of the Late Commerce Secretary, Malcolm Baldrige who did a lot to promote quality awareness in US industry. It cites as its purposes to *"promote quality awareness, to recognize quality achievement of US companies and to publicise successful strategies"*. Put in simple terms the award is designed to honour the companies that have shown the greatest commitment to quality improvement and management.[23]

The awards are given in three categories: manufacturing, service, and small business. No more than two awards per category can be awarded per year. The awards are managed by the US National Institute of Standard and Technology, an agency of the US Commerce Department's Technology Administration. The private sector is also actively involved in the award process.

The award examination items and scoring criteria form a comprehensive base for measuring a quality improvement process. The general examination categories are as follows:

1. Leadership
2. Information and Analysis

3. Strategic Quality Planning
4. Human Resource Utilisation
5. Quality Assurance of Products and Services
6. Results from Quality Assurance of Products and Services
7. Customer Satisfaction[24]

The full details of the Malcolm Baldrige National Award examination items and scoring criteria can easily be found on the internet. In 1988, the award's first year, 66 American companies applied for the awards that were eventually won by Motorola, Westinghouse, and Globe Metallurgical. The awards contain some excellent criteria for measuring the status of quality improvement efforts. A 1988 survey by The G.O.A.L/QPC organization of 130 of 1,000 US largest companies found that those companies aware of the award, and particularly those familiar with its criteria, tended to report much better result (in quality, cost and productivity) from their quality programmes. Badiru and Ayeni (1993) reported that in just a few years the MBNQA has become an important agent for transforming company attitudes towards quality from complacency to renewed enthusiasm.[25] At the time of our study, some 10 states in the US had their own quality awards patterned after the MBNQA.[26] The Minnesota Quality Award model, according to Badiru and Ayeni, has received national acclaim in the US because of its integrative approach.

Also in the US the Ishikawa Medal (named after Professor Kaoru Ishikawa, the "father of the quality circles") is awarded to companies for achievement of Outstanding Leadership in Advancing the Human Aspect of Quality by the ASQC. Instituted in 1993, the Eastman Chemical Company, a subsidiary of Eastman Kodak, became the first company to win the award that year.[27] In addition to companies, awards and prizes are also given to individuals who have made lasting contribution to the quality revolution. In the US they include the Shewart Medal, Edwards Medal, Williard F. Rockwell Medal, National Medal of Technology in America, Lancaster Award, Grant Award, Industrial Standardization Prize, all given out by the American Society for Quality Control and the International Technology Institute. [28]

Outside the US , The Deming Prize and the Nihon Keizai Press Prize are awarded in Japan . Also in Japan , the highest decoration presented to non-Japanese citizens is the Second Order of the Sacred Treasure by the Emperor of Japan. So far only W. Edwards Deming and Joseph M. Juran have been decorated for their contribution to the Japanese Quality revolution.[29]

Internationally, the International Quality Europe Award, which highlights Europe's prevailing focus on quality, is gaining wide acceptance from all over the world. Two of the awards for the1991 competition held in Madrid , Spain , went to two Nigerian Companies, Obokun Bola Dare Nigeria and South Coast Development Company Limited.[30]

THE QUALITY GURUS, THEIR IDEAS AND TEACHINGS

Professor Tony Bendell writing in the Department of Trade and Industry (DTI) booklet, **The Quality Gurus: What Can They Do For Your Company?**, quoting Roget, stated that *"a guru is a good man, a wise man and teacher".* A Quality Guru, according to Bendell, should be all of these, and in addition a *"charismatic individual whose concept and approach to quality within business and possible life generally, has made a major and lasting impact."* [31]

The DTI booklet was part of '**THE ENTERPRISE INITIATIVE: MANAGING IN THE 90S PROGGRAMME'**. According to Bendell, three clear groups of Quality Gurus can be identified covering the period since World War II. These are:

1. The early Americans who took the message to the Japanese. They include William Edwards Deming, Joseph M. Juran and Armand V. Feigenbaum. (Early 1950s).
2. The Japanese who developed new concepts in response to the Americans' message. They include Kaoru Ishikawa, Genichi Taguchi and Shigeo Shingo. (Late 1950 onwards)
3. The new western wave of Gurus who following Japanese industrial success, have given rise to increased quality awareness in the west. They include Philip B. Crosby, Tom Peters and Claus Moller. (1970-1980s)[32]

Below are the messages of the individual gurus.

WILLIAM EDWARD DEMING

Together with Joseph Juran, W. Edwards Deming is generally recognized as the father of the Total Quality Movement. He was decorated with the Second Order of The Sacred Treasure, the highest award given to a non-Japanese citizen by the Emperor of Japan in 1960, for his contribution to the Japanese Quality Revolution.

Here are Deming's 14 points for Management

1. Create constancy of purpose to improve product and service.
2. Adopt new philosophy for new economic age by management learning responsibilities and taking leadership for change.
3. Cease dependence on inspection to achieve quality; eliminate the need for mass inspection by building quality into products.
4. End awarding business on price; instead minimize total cost and move towards single suppliers for items.
5. Improve constantly and forever the system of production and service to improve quality and productivity and to decrease cost
6. Institute training on the Job.
7. Institute leadership; supervision should be to help do a better job; overhaul supervision of management and production workers.

8. Drive out fear so that all may work effectively for the organisation.

9. Break down barriers between departments; research, design sales and production must work together to foresee problems in production and use.

10. Eliminate slogans, exhortations and numerical targets for the workforce, such as 'zero defects' or new productivity levels. Such exhortations are diversory as the bulk of the problems belong to the system and beyond the power of the workforce.

11. Eliminate quotas or work standards, and management by objectives or numerical goals; substitute leadership.

12. Remove barriers that rob people of their right to pride of workmanship, hourly worker, management and engineering; eliminate annual or merit ratings and management by objective.

13. Institute a vigorous education and self improvement programme.

14. Put everybody in the company to work to accomplish the information.

In addition to the 14-point management plan, Deming also identified seven impediments to achieving quality transformation. These he called the 'deadly diseases.' Here they are.

Deming's 7 Deadly Diseases

Here we highlight only five of Deming's deadly diseases as two (excessive medical costs and excessive legal damage awards) are peculiar to American industrial companies. The five that are not include:

1. A lack of constancy of purpose.
2. Emphasis on short term profits etc.
3. Evaluation of performance, merit rating and annual review.
4. Mobility of management.
5. Management by use only of visible figures, with little or no consideration of unknown or unknowable figures.

Deming identified the obstacles that he saw in addition to these diseases as a range of attitudes which can get in the way of the necessary transformation e.g. 'hope for instant pudding' or 'our quality control department takes care of all our problems of quality'.

Deming advocated action based on a seven-point plan.

Deming's 7-point action plan

1. Management struggles over the 14 points, deadly diseases and obstacles and agrees meaning and plans direction
2. Management takes pride and develops courage for the new direction.

3. Management explains to the people in the company why change is necessary.

4. Divide every company activity into stages, identifying the customer of each stage as the next stage. Continual improvement of each stage should take place at each stage, and stages should work together toward quality.

5. Start as soon and as quickly as possible to construct an organization to guide continual quality improvement. Deming advocates the Deming or Shewhart Cycle as a helpful procedure for improvement of any stage.

6. Everyone can take part in any team to improve the input and output of any stage

7. Embark on construction of organization for quality. (Deming sees this as requiring the participation of knowledgeable statisticians).

In the 1980's, Deming attempted a summary of his 60 years' experience. This he called the '*System of Profound Knowledge*.' It described four interrelated parts:

1. **Appreciation for system.**

   This emphasizes the need for managers to understand the relationship between functions and activities. Everyone should understand that the long term aim is for everybody to gain - employees, shareholders, customers, suppliers, and the environment. Failure to accomplish the aim causes loss to everybody in the system.

2. **Knowledge of statistical theory**

   This includes knowledge about variation, process capability, control charts, interactions and loss function. All these need to be understood to accomplish effective leadership, teamwork, etc.

3. **Theory of knowledge**

   All plans require prediction based on past experience. An example of success cannot be successfully copied unless the theory is understood.

4. **Knowledge of psychology**

   It is necessary to understand human interactions. Differences between people must be used for optimization by leaders. People have intrinsic motivation to succeed in many areas. Extrinsic motivators in employment may smother intrinsic motivation. These include pay rises and performance grading, although these are sometimes viewed as a way out for managers.

JOSEPH M. JURAN

Like Deming, Juran was also decorated with the Second Order of the Sacred Treasures by the Emperor of Japan. Intrinsic in Juran's message is the belief that quality does not happen by accident, it must be planned. Juran sees quality planning as part of the quality trilogy of quality planning, quality control and quality improvement. He summarised the planning aspect in his 'Quality Planning Road Map' consisting of the following steps:

1. Identify who are the customers.
2. Determine the need of those customers.
3. Translate those needs into our language.
4. Develop a product that can respond to those needs
5. Optimize the product features so as to meet our need as well as the needs of the customer
6. Develop a process which is able to produce the product.
7. Optimize the process.
8. Prove that the process can produce the product under operating conditions
9. Transfer to operations

According to Juran, The mission of his recent work was:

1. Creating an awareness of the quality crises of the 1980s.
2. Establishing a new approach to quality planning, and training.
3. Assisting companies to re-plan existing processes avoiding quality deficiencies
4. Establish mastery within companies over the quality planning process thus avoiding the creation of new chronic problems.

Juran's formula for results is:
1. Establish specific goals to be reached.
2. Establish plans for reaching the goals.
3. Assign clear responsibility for meeting the goals.
4. Base rewards on results achieved.

ARMAND V. FEIGENBAUM.

Feigenbaum's message is in the form of ten crucial benchmarks for total quality success. These are that:
1. Quality is a companywide process.
2. Quality is what the customer says it is.
3. Quality and cost are a sum, not the difference.
4. Quality requires both individual and team zealotry.
5. Quality is a way of managing.
6. Quality and innovation are mutually dependent.
7. Quality is an ethic.
8. Quality requires continuous improvement.
9. Quality is the most cost effective, least capital-intensive route to productivity.
10. Quality is implemented with a total system connected with customers and suppliers.

KAORU ISHIKAWA

Ishikawa sees the Company-wide Quality Control movement as implying that quality does not only mean the quality of product, but also of after sale service, quality of management, the company itself and the human being. This has the effect that:

1. Product quality is improved and become uniform. Defects are reduced.
2. Reliability of goods is improved.
3. Cost is reduced.
4. Quality of product is increased, and it becomes possible to make rational production schedules.
5. Wasteful work and rework are reduced.
6. Technique is established and improved
7. Expenses for inspection and testing are reduced.
8. Contracts between vendor and vendee are rationalized.
9. The sales market is enlarged.
10. Better relationships are established between departments.
11. False data and report are reduced.
12. Discussions are carried out more freely and democratically.
13. Meetings are operated more smoothly.
14. Repairs and installation of equipment and facilities are done more rationally.
15. Human relations are improved.

PHILIP B. CROSBY

Crosby's quality process is based upon the **Four Absolutes of Quality management.**

1. Quality is defined as conformance to requirements, not as 'goodness' or 'elegance'.

2. The system for causing quality is prevention, not appraisal.
3. The performance standard must be Zero Defect, not 'that's close enough'
4. The measurement of quality is the Price of Non-conformance, not indices.

The fourteen steps to Quality Improvement are the way that the Quality Improvement Process is implemented in an organization. They are a management tool which evolved out of a conviction that the *Absolutes* should be defined, understood, and communicated in a practical manner to every member of the organization:

1. Make it clear that management is committed to quality.
2. Form quality improvement teams with senior representatives from each department.
3. Measure processes to determine where current and potential quality problems lie.
4. Evaluate the cost of quality and explain its use as a management tool.
5. Raise the quality awareness and personal concern of all employees.
6. Take actions to correct problems identified through previous steps
7. Establish progress monitoring for the improvement process.
8. Train supervisors to actively carry out their part in the quality improvement programme.

9. Hold a Zero Defects Day to let everyone know that there has been a change and to reaafirm management's commitment.
10. Encourage individuals to establish improvement goals for themselves and their groups.
11. Encourage employees to communicate to management the obstacles they face in attaining their improvement goals.
12. Recognise and appreciate those who participate.
13. Establish quality councils to communicate on a regular basis.
14. Do it all over again to emphasize that the quality improvement programme never ends.

Crosby later enunciated five new characteristics essential to becoming an *Eternally Sucessful Organisation.*
1. People routinely do things right the first time.
2. Change is anticipated and used to advantage.
3. Growth is consistent and profitable.
4. New products and services appear when needed.
5. Everyone is happy to work there.

TOM PETERS

Tom Peters is best known for his customer orientation. Concerning customer responsiveness, he describes *twelve attributes, or traits of a quality revolution.*

The twelve traits are:

1. **Management obsession with quality**

   This stresses the importance of practical action to back up the emotional commitment, e.g. halving the number of rework mechanics, never walking past shoddy goods.

2. **Passionate system**

   Failure is inviarable due to passion without system, or system without passion, Peter believes. Both are necessary and an ideology is needed whether based on Gurus or not

3. **Measurement of quality**

   This should begin at the outset of the programme, should be displayed, and should be carried out by the participants.

4. **Quality is rewarded**

   Quality based incentive compensation can cause early breakthrough in top management's attitude.

5. **Everyone is trained for quality**

   Everyone in the company should be extensively trained. Instructions in cause and effect analysis, statistical process control, group interaction should be given to all.

6. **Multi-funtion teams**

   Quality Circles (QC), Cross Functional Teams (CFT) such as Error Cause Removal or Correction Action Teams should be introduced. Based on his experience Peters favors cross functional teams.

7. **Small is beautiful**

   There is no such thing as small improvements. There is significance in the fact that change has occurred.

8. **Create endless ' Hawthorne' effects**

   This is the antidote to the 12-18 month doldrums. New goals, new teams, new events are the antidote.

9. **Parallel organization structure devoted to quality improvement**

   This describes creation of shadow quality teams and emphasizes that it is a route through which hourly paid workers can progress.

10. **Everyone is involved**

    Suppliers especially, but distributors and customers too, must be part of the organization's quality process. Joint improvement teams can be formed.

11. **When quality goes up, costs go down**

    Quality improvement is the primary source of cost reduction. The elementary force at work is the simplification design, process and procedures

12. **Quality improvement is a never-ending journey**

    All quality is relative. Each day each product is getting relative better or worse, but never stands still.

CLAUS MOLLER

Moller sees Personal Quality (PQ) as the basis of all other types of quality. He identifies two standards of personal quality. The ideal performance level (IP) and the actual performance level (AP). Improving the personal development of the individual will lead to increased competence in the three vital areas of Productivity, Relations and Quality.

Moller presents twelve Golden Rules to help improve the Actual performance level.

These are:

1. Set personal quality goals.
2. Establish your own personal quality account.
3. Check how satisfied others are with your effort.
4. Regard the next link as a valued customer.
5. Avoid errors.
6. Perform task more effectively.
7. Utilize resources well.
8. Be committed.
9. Learn to finish what you start - strengthen your self discipline.
10. Control your stress.
11. Be ethical – Maintain your integrity.
12. Demand quality.

Concerning company quality, Moller identifies *17 hallmarks of a quality company.* These are:

1. **Focus on quality development.**
   Quality development is just as much a part of company life as budgets and accounts.

2. **Management participation in the quality process.**

   Management visibly strives to meet the higher standards the program set for effeciency and human relations.

3. **Satisfied customers / users.**

   They remain loyal to the company.

4. **Committed Employees.**

   Employees thrives. Turnover and absenteeism are below normal.

5. **Long - term quality development.**

   The company invest more in long-term quality development than short- term profits.

6. **Clearly-defined quality goals.**

   Quality goals for all areas clearly defined, result are publicised.

7. **Quality performance rewarded.**

   Quality performance is rewarded visibly, and is a prerequisite for promotion.

8. **Quality control perceived positively.**

   Quality control is not perceived as assign of distrust, but rather as a means to develop and maintain quality.

9. **Next person in work process is a valued customer.**

   No link/person in the chain should suffer because of the mistakes made by others.

10. **Investment in personal training and development.**

Employees are the company's most important resource.

11. **Prevention/reduction of mistakes.**

Sizable investments are made to prevent and limit mistakes.

12. **Appropriate decision level.**

The level of decision-making is placed no higher in the organization than necessary.

13. **Direct route to end users.**

Products and services are delivered by the most direct method available.

14. **Emphasis on both technical and human quality.**

Every job has two dimensions, the technical and human dimension

15. **Company actions directed towards customer needs.**

Meeting the customer's needs is reflected in all company actions.

16. **Ongoing value analysis.**

Work which does not create value is dropped.

17. **Company recognition of its role in the society.**

The company assumes roles in contributing to society.

SOME UNIFYING PRINCIPLES AND CONCEPTS

After reviewing the works of the Quality Gurus for the period 1940 – 1991, Prof. Tony Bendell made the following summary of their message:

1. Management commitment and employee awareness are essential from early stages for implementing TQM. Deming's philosophy, Peters' top twelve traits, Crosby's Zero Defect and Moller's Personal Quality are possibly the most successful for encouraging these attitudes.

2. The awareness should be backed up by facts and figures. Planning and data collection are important. Cost of Quality can be used to measure the progress of improvement and Juran is perhaps the Guru who has played the most significant role in this area, although Crosby has contributed.

3. TQM programmes normally employ teamwork to facilitate improved communications and problem solving. Cross-functional teams are particularly advocated widely by Peters and Crosby, and can be very successful if other TQM structures are in place.

4. Simple tools for problem-solving and improvement such as Ishikawa methods should be learned and used by all employees.

5. Technical tools to control industrial design and manufacturing should be mastered. These include Taguchi methods, which can be used to reduce prototyping, and Shingo's work for successful Just-in-time systems.

6. Management tools should be studied to achieve quality. These include Crosby's Zero Defect approach, and the concepts of Companywide Quality and Total Quality Control associated with Ishikawa and Feigenbaum.

7. In order to move from an inspection to a prevention culture characteristic of TQM, emphasis is normally placed on the identification of internal customers and suppliers. This implies the understanding required to meet the external customers' requirement. This customer focus is probably emphasised most strongly by Juran, Crosby (internal customers), Peters and Deming's recent teachings (external customers).

Ronald M. Fortuna (1992), writing in **Total Quality: A Managers's Guide for the 1990s,** counsels that *"quality cannot be copied; there is no step-by-step cookbook that applies equally to all company situations and cultures."* [34]

He however identified what he called 15 'cohesive set of principles' which he listed as follows:
1. Customer first orientation.
2. Top management leadership of the quality improvement process.

3. Focus on continuous improvement.
4. Respect for employees and their knowledge; employees are actively involved in the improvement process.
5. Reduction of process and process variation.
6. Provision of ongoing education and training of employees.
7. Familiarity with a statistical way of thinking and the use of statistical methods throughout the organization.
8. Emphasis on prevention rather than detection.
9. View of vendors as long term partners.
10. Performance measures that are consistent with the goals of the organization.
11. Standardization – the development of and adherence to the best known ways to perform a given task.
12. Emphasis of product and service quality in design.
13. Cooperation and improvement of all functions within an organization.
14. Awareness of the needs of internal customers.
15. Substantial cultural change.

In emphasizing the need for total systems integration as one of the unifying principles of TQM, William H. Davidow and Bro Uttal (1989) in their **Total Customer Service: The Ultimate Weapon** warned practitioners when they said, "*though we have tried to simplify the elements of producing outstanding service, and their subsidiary principles, putting them into practice is never simple. On the other hand, all the elements hang together. The best infrastructure in the world is little* *more than a drag on profit if employees snarl at customers. The most elegant service strategy is so much hot air if it is not based on accurate measurement of customer expectations and corporate service performance. The most inspiring leadership cannot compensate for a product so poorly designed that it breaks down often and take forever to fix it".[35]*

As Aristotle observed, excellence is a habit, an attitude. We believe it is the attitudinal dimension that led Philip B Crosby (1989) to say that *"people hold the key to quality."* Crosby went on to say *"through the years, I have come to realize that there is a lot involved in running a company that has little to do with the content of management systems. It all has to do with people: if we take care of the customers and the employees everything else takes care of itself. It is hard to find an organization that both customers and employees regard with continuous affection and appreciation".[36]* Attention to people (internal and external) therefore is the most fundamental unifying principle in the whole quality management movement.

Excellent companies treal their employees exceptionally well, which is a factor in, and a result of, their success. Robert Haas, at the time the CEO of Levi Strauss Associate, equally emphasised that employee engagement and satisfaction are fundamental to running a strong business. Speaking to Fortune magazine (Fortune International February 8, 1993) he said, *"you have to create an environment where everyone feels like a representative of the company. Unless you have people who know what you stand for and want to make every transaction the best, you are going to stub your toe."* [37]

2.4.2 MYTHS AND MISCONCEPTIONS

Due to the all embracing nature of TQM and the bewildering variety of approaches, some myths and misconceptions have tended to detract from the subject. Lionel Stebbing (1989) highlighted some of the myths and misconceptions. According to Stebbing:

Quality assurance is not:
1. Quality control or inspection.
2. A super checking activity
3. Responsible for engineering decisions.
4. A massive paper generator
5. A major cost area
6. A panacea for all ills.

Stebbing then went on to say what quality assurance is:
1. Cost effective
2. An aid to productivity.
3. A means of getting it right, first time, everytime.
4. A good management sense.
5. The responsibility of everyone.[38]

BARRIERS TO QUALITY

Laura A. Liswood (1991), a one time Senior Examiner for the Malcolm Baldrige National Quality Award and Author of the book **Serving Them Right**,[39] listed 10 barriers to the achievement of quality in an organization. Here they are:

1. The differences in people.
2. Believing that customers are expendable.
3. Unwillingness to pay the price.
4. Supervised commitment.
5. Listening but not hearing , looking but not seeing.
6. Using assembly line principles for service delivery.
7. Quality service is hard to define and measure.
8. The protective shield of policies, procedures and protocol.
9. Preoccupation with short-term results.
10. Overselling

Liswood acknowledged the above list was not exhaustive.

John MacDonald (1993) of the British Institute of Management in his book **Understanding Total Quality Management In A Week**[40], listed ten reasons why TQM fail.
They are:

1. A lack of management commitment.
2. A lack of vision and planning.
3. A satisfaction with the quick fix.
4. The process of change became tool bound.
5. The word quality became constraining.
6. The culture change and project approach became conflicting.
7. Quality management became bureaucratic.
8. Management did not change its behaviour.

9. The people were not really involved.
10. A lack of business measurables to measure TQM.

Many barriers always stand on the way of quality, the chief among which is the habitual unwillingness of people to change. One aspect of this attitude is the constant view by the majority of executives in organisations that their number one problem is finance and not quality. In this context *Quality* is equated to quality control, which is of course is quite different. The aim of *Quality* is to make Quality Control superfluous. A change in behavior therefore is the necessary starting point for the implementation of any *Quality* improvement programme.

Robert Galvin then of Motorola recalled that when Motorola began to formulate its new Quality Programme, there was strong resistance. " *Motorola was number one in our industry in market share, sales and profit at the same time. However our product quality really stunk, and we had to do something about it. But people said we shouldn't spend our time and money on such a thing. That happened to be during the hard times of 1978, and many of our officers thought we should be concentrating on day to day concerns like sales and finance."* Galvin went on to say, *"people wanted to talk about everything but Quality. They didn't relate Quality to other operations and issues such as finance and sale".*[41]

The experience of many other companies is not dissimilar to Motorola's. People always fail to see the causal relationship between Quality and other functions. The first step in Quality programme is to break down all the barriers to Quality.

The story of Motorola had a happy ending. The company embarked on its Quality journey in 1978 and became one of the first companies to win the MBNQA when it was established in 1988. The company had annual sales of US$11billon in 1988 when it won the award. In the 1990s the company started embarking on what it called 'virtual perfection'. It hoped to make only 3.4 defective parts per million. This is the so called 'Six Sigma' approach to quality. Six Sigma means six standard deviations from statistical performance average. The Sigma Six approach allows for no more that 3.4 defects per million parts in manufactured goods or 3.4 mistakes per million activities in a service operation. The decline of Motorola relative to Nokia and Samsung emphasises the all important fact that Quality per say is not a cure all for all ailments.[42] Motorola blew its chances of becoming masters of the new digital revolution when its Iridium project went belly up, allowing Samsung to overtake it in 2009 in the GSM telephone segment.

Chapter Three

QUALITY: WHY DOES IT MATTER?

The terms *Quality* and *Excellence* are nowadays used interchangeably though in recent times Excellence has tended to predominate unlike the 70's and 80's when Quality was all the rave. The term *Excellence* became popular with the release in 1978 of the book **In Search of Excellence: Lessons from America's Best-Run Companies** by Tom Peters and Robert H. Waterman Jr. National Public Radio in 1999 placed the book among the "Top Three Business Books of the Century," and a poll by Bloomsbury Publishing in 2002 ranked it as the "greatest business book of all time". The book, which was also ranked by Warner Books as the "best selling business book of all time", has spawned hundreds of other books on the subject of *Excellence,* which combined, have raised awareness about *Quality* not only in US and Europe, but globally. No company can hope to survive today for long with mediocre service, thanks to the internet and globalisation so like it or not quality matters. And also thanks to the internet and globalisation, like it or not, yours is a global business. Martha Rogers, at the time a partner at Peppers and Rogers Group reminded business people and readers in **The Conference Board** article: One Customer at a Time: Competing in the Interactive Age to brace up for competition as

"Everybody everywhere wants your most valuable customers and will approach them from all channels and geographies in ways unimaginable just a few years ago. So, like it or not, yours is a global enterprise."

In Search was replete with stories of how employees in some of the cited excellent companies went all out to *die* for the customer. In one of the numerous graphic examples, the book tells the story of how workers in Frito Lay, then a subsidiary of the Pepsi Cola Company, braced snow, sleet, mud, hail and storm to service customers all in their brave bid to uphold the company's service record.[1] Such is the emotional appeal total quality has on people when it takes hold. Globally it has been recognized that the process of continuous improvement (kaizen in Japanese), the hallmark of the Total Quality Movement, has been the key to Japan's economic ascendancy, and lately China and South Korea. In a relatively short period of 40 years from the end of the Second World War, the Japanese have taken over and now dominate so completely certain markets that were previously the exclusive preserve of American and European companies. These include steel, shipbuilding, cars, cameras, watches, television and other household entertainment electronics, to mention a few. Names such as Toyota , Honda, Toshiba, Sanyo, Sony to mention a few, are now household names worldwide. The success of Japanese industries cannot be separated from their close attention to Quality.[2] Juran (1961) predicted the Japanese miracle.

So what is *Quality* all about and what are the pay offs? Total Quality Management is a concept that has emerged as a way to achieve systems approach to quality management. Total Quality Management refers to total commitment to *Quality*. Total in this sense refers to an overall integrated approach to all aspects of quality, considering all the people, all the hardware, all the software, and all the organizational resources. Quality management involves an integrated management of all the functions that can impact the quality of a product (or service). Summarizing the essence of Total Quality Management, Badiru and Ayeni gave this important clarification, *"Quality Assurance sets the standard for product [and service] quality while Quality Control implements or enforces those standards. Quality Management oversees and integrates all functions that can influence quality."* [3]

TQM is a comprehensive system for achieving continuous improvement in customer satisfacstion. It is a philosophy of total integration of the business to achieve the required result. The goal is to achieve greater effectiveness and efficiency, lower operating cost, and increased market share. TQM practices focus on satisfying customer needs. This means making the needs of the customer the priority, expanding the relationship beyond traditional services and incorporating the customer's needs in the company's business plan and corporate strategy. For top Management, TQM means improving the internal financial and operational management of the company thereby better serving the needs of all stakeholders. [4]

Ronald M. Fortuna (1992) writing in the same vein emphasised that *"what we mean by Quality is more than the tradidtional notion of quality of products or services. Our definition simultaneously encompasses improvement in cost positions, delivery performance, time taken to get products unto the market, and responsiveness to changes in the market-place. It is a bottom line issue that addresses the very roots of a business, and it requires a change in thinking from the top of the organization to the bottom."* [5]

TQM means changing the way people do things so as to minimize the potential for errors or defects. The TQM approache uses statistical methods to find problems that cause errors or defects. The TQM philosophy is so called because as Mike Robson pointed out in his video film The Journey to Excellence:

1. It involves everybody in the organization.
2. It involves every single piece of work done in the organization.
3. It require total [management] commitment. [6]

Badiru and Ayeni (1993) used the business-customer integration loop to explain the TQM approach. Quality system intergration requires that the business looks out for the customer while the customer also looks out for the survival of the business, for, if there is no business, there will be no product, and if there is no product, customers' needs cannot be met. If customers are satisfied, they will be more willing to embrace the products offered by the business thereby creating further profit potential for the business. A business in this virtuous cycle will inevitably achieve unending success. [7]

Denis Walker (1990) who helped design the strategy underpinning the *Customer First* campaign at the British Airway pointed out, *"Customers are constantly measuring actual or perceived service against the image you are projecting and the promises you are making. They are also telling other potential customers of their experience and creating their expectations and prejudices."*[8] He advised that *"If customer service really differentiates you from your competitors, you need to tell your customers about it. But it you cannot match your own propaganda, you will not be treated kindly in the marketplace."*[9] He then went on to situate customer expectation within the context of company advertising campaign. *"Advertising raises customer expectations to a certain level. If the product or service meets those expectations, the market position is strengthened, but at the same time, customers expect even better service next time. If services fail to meet expectations, then customers are dissatisfied, particularly when an advertising campaign has promised them something better. Staff morale suffers and economic performance declines."* [10]

Numerous research have established the strong relationship between quality and business success. One of the most extensive studies carried out and that has established conclusively the strong connection between quality and business performance was the Profit Impact of Market Strategies (PIMS) studies by Buzzell and Gale (1987). Buzzell and Gale noted that *"there is no doubt that relative perceived quality and profitability are strongly related. Whether the profit measure is return on sales or return on investment, business with a superior product service offering clearly outperform those with inferior quality. Market share is the key to a company's growth and profitability, and one factor above all others – quality drives market share. And when superior quality and large market share are both present, profitability is virtually guaranteed".[11]* According to Buzzell and Gale there are two basic ways to beat competitors. *"One is to achieve superior perceived quality by developing a set of product specification and service standards that more closely meet customer need than competitors. The other is to achieve superior conformance quality by being more effectve than other competitors in conforming to appropriate product specifications and service standards."[12]* Buzzell and Gale emphasized that the two ways of winning are not mutually exclusive and advised companies to strive to outperform their competitors on both perceived quality and conformance quality. Focusing on achieving superior perceived quality they highlighted gives businesses three options, including the ability to charge a higher price thus gaining a higher profit, charging a higher price and investing the premium in Research and Development and in new products to ensure the perceived quality and market share for the future, and finally, offering the customer better value by charging the same price as competitors. If the third option is adopted, this will allow the firm to build for the future by gaining market share, resulting in volume growth, rising capacity utilization, and ultimately allowing you to introduce new equipment that embodies the lastest cost-saving technology. According to Buzzell and Gale, achieving superior conformance quality yields two key benefits, including lower *cost of quality* than that of competitors thereby a lower overall cost. More tellingly, conformance quality influences purchase decisions, thus leading to lower cost and superior perceived quality. Quality positively impacts not only profitability, but also growth, the other key dimension of business performance through the impact of quality on perceived value. According to Buzzell and Gale, *''value is the relationship between quality and price. A customer who gets superior quality at a low price gets better value; a customer who gets inferior quality at higher price obviously gets worst value. In a competitive market, it is the customer who determines what constitutes a good or poor quality, high or low price. Who he buys from, and at what price, determines who wins or loses.''*[13] In driving home the point on the primacy of the customer's view on what constitutes quality and value, Buzzell and Gale concluded, saying *''quality is whatever the customer says it is, and the quality of a particular product or services is whatever the customer perceives it to be.''*[14] By comparing your offering with those of competitors, the customer decides whether a particular offering represents superior or inferior quality, or a high or low price.

In their study, those businesses in the top 20 ranking for perceived relative quality had an average return on investment of over 30 per cent, nearly double that of companies in the buttom 20 percentile. Return followed a similar pattern. Buzzell and Gale concluded that *"this performance gap flows from the benefits that businesses reap from having higher perceived quality in the market Place: stronger customer loyalty, more repeat purchases, less vulnerability to price wars, ability to command higher relative price without affecting share, lower marketing cost, and share improvements."* [15]

A summary of the PIMS data yielded three vital lessons:

1. Companies rated better than average with respect to service were able to charge around 9 per cent more than those rated below average.
2. The better companies expanded their market share by 6 per cent per annum
3. The lower rated companies experienced a 2 per cent annual decline in market share.

The relationship between financial performance and customer satisfaction holds true in service-oriented businesses as well. For instance, the Technical Assistance Research Programme (TARP) Instittue in the US reported that each customer retained by a bank for more than five years equated to roughly $263 (N39,450) in profit. [16]

A summary of the TARP research findings is highlighted as follows:

1. 26 out of 27 people having a bad service experience do not report i.e. only about 4 per cent actually complain.
2. 91 per cent of those who don't complain don't come back.
3. On average though, they tell 9 - 10 colleagues about it.

4. 13 per cent tell more than 20 people
5. 90 per cent return if "saved" by a well handed recovery.[17]

The service company that shuns its complaining customers is taking a very short term view. According to Laura Liswood, *"losing a customer usually has a 'domino effect' which is poorly understood or not recognized at all by management."*[18] Surveys by the American Society for Quality Control (ASQC) and the Gallup Organization (1988) also suggested a strong relationship between quality and price realization. Survey respondents indicated that they were willing to pay substantial premiums for higher quality goods over the baseline price for the same goods of "average" quality.[19] In a Mckinsey & Company survey "**Customer Satisfaction Versus Repurchase Intent**" 85 per cent of customers who were satisfied with sales and services expressed the intent to repurchase from the same dealer compared to 1 per cent by dissatisfied customers. In another McKinsey survey, 36 per cent of respondents said they would switch banks because of poor service compared to other factors such as high fees (32 per cent), long lines at window (28 per cent), and errors on statements (22 per cent). In yet another survey by McKinsey titled "**Why industrial Companies Lose Customers**" company indifference was cited as the most important reason for leaving (68 per cent), while other factors such as lower price [else where], and relocation, to mention a few, ranked far below at 9 per cent and 3 per cent respectively. [20]

There is ample evidence in the literature to confirm the positive contribution of the focus on *Quality* to business performance. Here are some further examples. The company JWS Technologies saw their late delivery drop from over 300 to below 10 within six months after implementing a TQM programme.[21] Also International Business Machine (IBM), the computer giant saw its products defect rate drop sharply after embracing total quality. [22] Similarly between 1987 and 1990, the Wallace Corporation in Texas increased its sales by more than 75 per cent, from $52mm to $90mm; market share rose from 10.4 per cent to 18 per cent; operating profit increased 7.4 times, after the company embraced TQM. The company went on to win the MBNQA in 1990.[23]

From the experience of world class companies, it is clear that high quality and low cost can be achieved simultaneously. This is certainly contrary to the conventional wisdom that higher quality can only be achieved through higher cost, such as for increased inspection. This again points to an expanded view of quality as *a way of doing business* rather than as a tactical objective and are determined long before manufacturing. Research by TARP indicated that only about a third of all instances of customer dissatisfaction were traceable to production problems. In the world class quality companies, costs are lower because customer requirements are best known, reducing the need for redesign and engineering and for expensive solutions to customer problems. Designs are optimized before production, further reducing manufacturing costs. Higher quality in the field is not coincidental to lower costs. It goes hand in hand with a low internal rate of defects, scrap and rework.

Regardless of the exact definition of quality, quality and satisfaction are determined ultimately by the customer's perception of a total product's value or service relative to its competition. As Berry pointed out *"customers expectations about levels of service are entirely reasonable"*. Bendell quoted Philip B. Crosby as saying in his book **Quality Is Free** that manufacturing companies spend 20 per cent of their revenues doing things wrong and doing them again. According to Crosby this can be 35 per cent of operating expenses for service companies. [24]

Certainly, the economics of Total Quality are totally compelling. The specutacular economic growth of Japan and other countries of the Pacific Rim has been attributed in part to their relentless pursuit of Quality, which was erroneously ascribed initially to *Eastern cultural values*, by companies in the West. The phrase '*The Customer Is King*' may sound hackneyed, but like it or not, nations, states, cities, corporations, agencies, and individuals run away from Quality at their own peril. As

Buzzell and Gale put it 'Quality is King'. Despite the compelling evidence, how did Union Bank Nigeria Plc., a bank founded in 1917, and boasting the tallest building on the Lagos Marina miss the Quality boat? A review of the basic approaches to managing quality service which will shed light on where Union Bank got it all wrong now follows.

Chapter Four

GRAPPLING WITH SERVICE MANAGEMENT

As a lawyer would say, a service has neither a body to kick nor a soul to damn. A service is nothing more than an intangible *solution* or even an experience that is provided to a customer. Kotler (1988) defined service as *"any act or performance that one party can offer to another that is essentially intangible and does not result in the ownership of anything. Its production may not be tied to a physical product."* [1] Companies offer to the market place range from pure tangible goods to pure services. A pure service offer consists primarily of a service. Services differ as to whether they are people-based or equipment based and as to whether they meet a personal need(personal service) or a business need (business service).

As a consequence of the varying goods-to-service mix, it is difficult to generalize about services unless some further distinctions are made. Here are some commonly held perceptions of what makes a service different from a product.

1. Sales, production and consumption of a service take place almost simultaneously.

2. A service cannot be centrally produced, inspected, stockpiled or wharehoused. It is usually delivered to wherever the customer is, by people who are beyond the immediate influence of management.

3. A service cannot be demonstrated, nor can a sample be sent for customer approval or trial in advance of purchase. The provider can explain, promise and tell how this service has benefitted others but the service doesn't exist for the prospective customer.

4. The person receiving the service generally owns nothing tangible once the service has been delivered. The value is frequently internal to the ciustomer.

5. A service is frequently an experience that cannot be shared, passed around or given away to someone else once it is delivered.

6. The more people there are in the delivery of service, the less likely it is the receiver will be satisfied.

7. The receiver of the service usually has a critical role to perform in the actualization of the service. The customers, then have to know their role in the delivery process.

8. Delivery of the service usually requires some form of human contact. The receiver and deliverer frequently come into contact in some relatively personal way.

9. The receivers' expectations are critical to their satisfaction with the service. What they get compared or contrasted to what they expected to get determines satisfaction.

10. Exerting quality control over a service requires monitoring of processes and attitudes.

From the foregoing we note that service differs from tangible products in four key characteristics, namely:

1. *Intangibility* Unlike physical products, they cannot be seen, tasted, felt heard, held, or smelled before they are bought.

2. *Inseparability* Unlike physical goods that are manufactured, stored and sold later, services are typically produced and consumed at the same time. It is difficult to separate the service provider from the service. If the service is rendered by a person, then the person is part of the service. Since the client is also present as the service is being produced, both the provider and the client affect the service.

3. *Variability* Services are highly variable as they depend on who provides them and when and where and how they are provided.

4. *Perishability* Service cannot be stored

To some extent managing service quality is more difficult because some elements are intangible and difficult to measure. A survey of service employees by the company, Inset Systems Company of Brookfield, Connecticut, (The Inserter, 1992) concerning what 'Quality' means in terms of job performance yielded the following responses:

'Providing extremely polite, prompt, and accurate service.'

'Viewing the customer as having done us a favor by buying our product'.

'Knowing as much as possible about products in order to support them better.'

'Researching problems to come up with good, solid solutions.'

'Maintaining good relationships with distributors and dealer to make customers feel comfortable.'

'Giving your all and going all out to *die* for the customer.'

'Providing customers with simple solutions to enable them do their work more efficiently.' [2]

Despite the difficulty in defining service and measuring some service elements, one advantage of managing service quality can be that a greater percentage of a company's employees are in contact with the external customer, therefore customer orientation can be made easier to achieve. This increased customer contact has been described as the 'moments of truth' by Jan Carlson, then president of the Scandinavian Airlines Systems (SAS). He said each time customers come into contact with an organization, they form an impression; each time is a *moment of truth*. The sum of the moments of truth forms the overall company quality rating. To be successful, companies need to manage the moments of truth so that a good quality impression is formed to ensure customers come back.[3]

Berry and his colleagues in 1985 developed a list of major determinants of service quality. They found that customers use basically similar criteria regardless of the type of service.[4] The criteria are summarised as follows:

1. **Access**: This refers to the receptiveness of the service provider to the customers request; the service is easy to access in convenient locations at convenient times with little waiting.
2. **Courtesy**: The employees are friendly, respectful, polite, considerate, empathetic.
3. **Competence**: This refers to the adequacy of skills and knowledge required to deliver service by employees.
4. **Communication**: This refers to the ability to listen to the customer, keep the customer informed, describe the service accurately in the customer's language and accept customer feedback.
5. **Credibility**: The company and employees are honest, trustworthy and have the customer's best interest at heart.
6. **Reliability**: This deals with the consistency, accuracy, and dependability of service.
7. **Responsiveness**: The employees respond quickly, willingly, promptly and creatively to customer's request

and problems. Responsiveness encompasses timeliness.

8. **Understanding**: Otherwise termed comprehension, this refers to the readiness of the service provider and all employees to know the customer, understand the customer's needs and provide individual attention.
9. **Security**: The service is free from danger, risk or doubt.
10. **Tangibles (Tools)**: This deals with the appearance of physical facilities, equipment, personnel, and communication materials.

Laura Liswood (1991) added the following customer wants:

1. Personal Treatment: Not becoming a statistic.
2. Price/Value legitimacy: Getting what you pay for.

Various studies of excellently managed service companies show that they share a number of common practices with respect to service quality. Among them are the following:

1. **A history of top management commitment to quality**: Companies such as Marriott, Disney, Delta, and McDonald have thorough commitment to quality. Their management look not only at financial performance on a monthly basis but also at service performance. Ray Kroc of McDonalds insisted on continually measuring each McDonald's outlet on its conformance to QSCV, namely, quality, service,

cleanliness and value. Franchisers that failed to conform were dropped.

2. **The setting of high standards**: the best service providers set high service standards. In the 1980s for instance, Swissair aimed for 96 per cent or more of its passengers rating its service as good or superior; otherwise it took action.

3. **Systems for monitoring service performance**: the top service companies audit service performance, both their own and competitors' on a regular basis. They use a number of devices to measure performance: comparison shopping, ghost shopping, mystery shopping, customer surveys, and suggestion and complaint forms. GE sends out seven hundred thousand cards a year to households to rate its service people performance. Citigroup checks continuously on measures of ART, namely, accuracy, responsiveness and timeliness. It does ghost shopping to check on its employees delivering good service

4. **Satisfying the employees as well as the customers**: Excellently managed service companies believe that employee relations will reflect on customer relations. Management creates an environment of employee support and rewards for good service performance. Management regularly audits employees satisfaction with their jobs.

Parasuraman, Zeithaml and Berry (1985) formulated a service quality model that highlighted the main requirement for a service provider delivering the expected service quality. The model identified five gaps that caused unsuccessful service delivery.[7] The first gap highlighted the "Gap between consumer expectation and management perception", which highlighted that management does not always perceive correctly what customers want or how customers judge the service components. For example, hospitals may focus on taste of food whereas patients may be more concerned with nurse responsiveness. The second gap is that "between management perception and service quality specifications", which has to do with standards set by management which may or may not be clear, realistic or unrealistic, or management may not be fully committed to enforcing the specified quality level. For example, "an airlines management may want phones to be answered within ten seconds of ringing but not provide enough operators nor do much about it when service fall below this level." On the third level is the "gap between service quality specifications and service delivery". This gap may be caused by poor training, overwork, low morale or equipment breakdowns. Operations' emphasis on efficiency may run counter to a drive for customer satisfaction. For example, a bank teller may be required by operations department to work fast while marketing department may direct all tellers to be courteous and friendly to each customer. The fourth is the "gap between service delivery and external communications". Heightened customer expectation caused by adverts not matched by service levels. For instance hotel rooms looking gorgeous in a brochure but quite cheap and stuffy looking in reality. The fifth and final is the "gap between perceived service and expected service". According to Berry et. al, *"this gap results when one or more of the previous gaps occur. It becomes clear why service providers have a hard time delivering the expected service quality."* [8]

A fundamental change in the culture of the organization is required to sustain long term quality improvement. Changes in the corporate culture in turn demand more than executive support or involvement. They necessitate leadership by example, objective analysis, the courage to take risks and allocate money, a willingness to share responsibility and rewards with employees, and an intense commitment to the ideal of creating new value and satisfaction for customers. Robert Galvin, the then Chairman of Motorola, made it clear that the commitment has to be *"deeply personal"* and that real change won't take palce until this personal feeling is transmitted throughout the ranks. And John C. Marous the then Chairman of Westinghouse Electric added that *"total quality is a cultural change which requires an emotional experience".* Laura A. Liswood pinpointed that *"strong leadership is the crucial ingredient required to create and sustain a quality culture. The leadership must completely embrace the quality process in everything it and its organization does."* [9]

Managing quality customer service as Carl Sewell (1992) pointed out requires the key elements of *"strategy, systems, standards, staff, communication, coordination, cooperation and measurement."* [10] A quality service strategy, Sewell made it clear *"must be guided by a compelling vision, built around customers priorities, communicated through out the organization and be subjected to frequent and formal measurement."[11]* He went on to say " *customer oriented systems are designed for the convenience of the customers; constantly reviewed, provide the customer with added value and allow swift and efficient recovery."[12] "Quality staff",* according to Sewell, *"have the following characteristics: they are carefully selected; undergo excellent training; are empowered to work for the customer and are generously rewarded."[13]*

On the whole, pro-active tools of assessment as essential elements of the improvement strategies are needed. The techniques listed below are representative of the sort of proactive methods from which an organization should select an approximate mix and develop its own strategies. To devise a strategy for service you need to:

1. Have a vision of the sort of experience you want the customers to have.
2. Have a vision of how the service strategy will make a difference.
3. Express your core purpose in a mission statement and communicate it to your staff.
4. Know your customers, their needs and satisfaction levels.
5. Understand how service can be used to create a competitive edge.
6. Know why some customers choose to use your competitors.

7. Build an organization designed to respond to the customer.
8. Develop systems which ensure quality of your product, service, environment and delivery.
9. Create a climate in which staff wish to respond to cutomer needs and provide them with the skills and knowledge to do so.
10. Establish people systems, policies and procedures which facilitate excellent service.

Tony Ansell (1993), at the time Head of Quality Assurance, Banking Operations, Midland Bank, pointed out that applying quality in the financial services industry is not just a matter of taking the techniques developed in other industries and using them without change. There are some important differences that need to be understood, amongst them:

1. Customers are usually suppliers as well as buyers.
2. Many areas require cooperation with competitors to complete, example, money transmission.
3. Customers often have only a very limited understanding of what they are buying.
4. Most banks are large integrated companies with central purchasing and relationship management for large clients.
5. Manufactured goods can have tolerance level, money must be accurate (a customer would not be pleased if he paid in $1,000 and found his account credited for

$999.99k an error of only 0.001 per cent - being close is not enough).[14]

Managing quality customer service in the banking industry is difficult but it is certainly attainable. The first step in that journey is the need to pay great attention to details. According to Laura Liswood, *"bank management thinks in terms of hundreds of million of dollars and tens or hundreds of thousands of customers, but that one customer whose cheques are bouncing because a deposit did not get credited is thinking in equally great terms on a personal level. To the bank manager, a $100 returned cheque may seem trivial; to the customer, it can mean the difference between good or bad credit rating."*[15] Liswood then zeroed in on the cashier who sees nothing wrong with long queues. To the cashier she said, *"a long queue may be a normal way of doing banking business, to the customer, it may be the difference between meeting and losing an appointment."* [16] Liswood we earlier pointed out was a one time examiner for the Malcolm Baldridge National Quality Awards. According to her, *"the issue is customer empathy."*[17] She concluded by saying *"Many banks are so caught up in their internal policies, procedures and systems that managers or frontline employees forget or never learn, how to be empathetic toward the customer. For that matter, the delivery chain itself may contain built-in-barriers to empathy."* [18]

In the delivery of a product or service there is a chain of events cutting across departmental boundaries which need to be diagrammed and continuously audited to ensure that all its links are in place. Someone, should have an overview of how the chain fit together and be in the position to predict where brakes may occur. This is nowadays called Business Process Management or Mapping (BPM) or Business Process Re-engineering (BPR). This involves re-examining the fundamental ways in which the business is operated. Re-engineering is a more relevant phrase as it involves taking processes to pieces and building a better, different, more effective process that more closely meets the objectives of the customer and the business. Though reingeneering is now regarded as a fad that has had its day, Michael Hammer's book, co-authored with James Champy, **Reingeneering The Cooperation,** was an instant hit when it came out in 1993, and was on the New York Times best seller list for 41 weeks, earning Dr. Hammer inclusion in Time magazine's list of "America's 25 Most Influential People" for 1996, do not overlook the importance of continually tinkering with your delivery processes to better serve the customer. The story how TSB (Trustee Savings Bank) in the UK re-engineered itself from a drab mediocre bank for retirees into a financial powerhouse of note is apt in this regard.

In the Trustee Savings Bank, their BPM consisted of six phases as reported by Peter Ellwood, (1993), Group Chief Executive, TSB Group. These were;

1. Identifying, mapping and costing the core business processes.
2. Selecting the process on which to work and establishing stretching goals for their redesign.

3. Conducting a detailed analysis of the process, asking fundamental questions like "what does the customer want?" and "what would we have to do to be, and be seen as the best?"

4. Radically redesigning the process by simplifying and rationalizing.

5. Managing the change closely to ensure that real benefits are obtained.

6. Establishing measurement and improvement programmes to ensure that the process continues to improve.[19]

In a paper presented at the 21st Cambridge Seminar of The Chartered Institute of Bankers, London, (now Institute of Financial Services –IFS), held at Christ College , Cambridge, in September 1993, Peter Ellwood whose bank was implementing TQM boasted: *"We have already identified and mapped 54 key processes, including their associated costs for our business. The first process we selected for redesign was home buying, because it incorporates major contact with the customer. Even the first measurements we made showed that there was considerable waste which could be avoided thereby removing hassles both within TSB and for our customers."* [20] Let's look at what TSB did in a little bit more detail. They did not just beem searchlight on mortgage application turnaround time, they drilled down to the questions in the mortgage loan application form and what they found made them quite uncomfortable. Peter Ellwood stated *''The average turnaround time from mortgage application to formal offer was 30 days. With less than one third achieved within 20 days. It took an average of four to five interviews with the customer to achieve completion, and there were five forms covering 167 questions of which only 24 were unique – for instance we asked them to fill in their account number no less than seven times. Not only was this an inefficient process, it also put us at some competitive disadvantage for a key product area."*[21] While the bank took comfort in the fact that in the year to October 1992, they grew mortgage balances at a rate two and a half times the rate of national market growth, and in six months to April 1993 this rose four times the rate of national market growth without detracting from credit quality or watering down their criteria for lending, which remained in line with those of the competition, Ellwood acknowledged that *"clearly the strength of the products and our promotion of them have made up for more than any deficiencies in the processing. But I also suspect that the issues we have identified are not unique within the industry or indeed to the home buying process."*[22] At the end of it all, TSB's redesigned processes cut total cost of mortgage processing by more than 25 per cent, the customer needed to complete only one greatly simplified form, and sign her signature just once. Peter Ellwood concluded, *"We believe we have proved the principle of BPM, and we are now carrying this sort of analysis forward to other parts of the business."* [23]

Having mapped out the chain the question arises, at what point is it more likely that a customer can become dissatisfied? You may wish to know that it does not require complex calculations to establish the weak links in the service delivery chain. What is needed is the organisation's willingness to see things from the customer's viewpoint. Seeking and understanding customers' requirements and putting in place a system for regular customer feedback is therefore the necessary starting point. Laura Liswood (1991) suggested using simple devices such as telephone surveys, mail surveys (with pre-paid envelopes), in-house suggestions boxes, mystery shoppers, focus group, mail "intercept" interviews; interactive video systems, in detecting how the customer feels.[24]

Another is the willingness of the top management to put in place an organization that encourages employees to constantly question *"the way we do things around here"*.[25] Bland statements that *"constructive criticism"* is welcome is never enough. Such gimmicks, as Liswood pointed out can even be counterproductive if employees sense unwillingness on the part of the management to effect changes in the way things are carried out despite management's claimed intentions. Liswood used the the experience most bank customers normally have on Friday afternoons to buttress her point. *''The typical scene is usually the long lines of frustrated customers. What the banks in these cases fail to recognise or refuse to accept is their own responsibility for repairing this weak link in their service chain. With these same Friday afternoon scenes recurring week in and week out , year in and year out, its about time somebody in the bank said 'we have got a service problem. All these customers cannot always be wrong. They must be trying to tell us something' ".[26]* As Liswood concluded,

''To ask these sort of questions and initiate an action process of change requires courage''. [27]

With globalisation, banking processes across the world, including China, India, USA, Nigeria, you name it are standardised and are basically universal. A typical banking relationship, Liswood summarised, involves the basic processes of opening the account, running or servicing the account and closing the account. In between you have account statements, returned cheques, opening and closing hours, forms used, information about available services, mistakes and errors, procedures to control queues or lines and to direct the customer how the account should be operated. Liswood lamented, *''sometimes you have a customer who has diligently operated his account for five to eight years and has his cheque bounced for minor infringement without attempt to find out if there was a death in the family or something happened that took him away from his normal routine. Somebody in the bank may blame the computer for such lapses but the customer's loyalty to your company may be suddenly and seriously diminished.''* [28] The message you have sent to the customer as Liswood pointed out is *"we are interested in you when all is well, we do not really appreciate your loyalty, in fact we don't even know about it."*[29]

Organizations and their employees always have to be alert to the customer-satisfaction implications of all their company's standard procedures and policies. There are a number of simple but effective actions that will show the customer that the bank really cares about what happens to them. Liswood suggested for example that somebody can call the customer the day after the cheque booklet was supposed to arrive and ask whether the booklet arrived and if the cheques were printed correctly. After the first statement is sent, somebody can call and ask whether it is accurate and if the customer needs anything explained. On the first anniversary of the account opening, a phone call or letter might ask: *"Are you pleased with our services? What can we do better? Can we advise you on anything involving finances or perhaps help you with some major purchases you are planning to make?"* [30]

True, these days almost all banks in Nigeria send birthday, Christmas, Eid-il- Kabir cards, and sometimes customised souvinirs to its important customers and members of their families. With advances in information technology it is now very easy to have a 360-degree view of every customer that would allow services to be more finely tailored to their needs but so long as banks continue to use technology only for their convenience there will always be problems.   For instance, almost all banks in Nigeria expect the customer to use the ATM if s/he wishes to withdrawing below N5,000, about $33.33, from his/her account thus depriving the customer of human contact. To show they mean business your account is debited for N1,000, about $6.66, if you go against the "law" of not using the ATM to make small withdrawals. To make the matter worse, if you stay too long in some banks you are promptly reminded you have overstayed your welcome by the security guards. Banks should beware that there is a body of research that suggests that most elderly bank customers visit their banks for human contact and company not just to withdraw cash so when they are denied of this psychological aspect of the relationship by the bank via technology and "policies", it can be devastating.

Deming (1982) pointed out, and Beskett (1994) confirmed that it is no longer adequate to satisfy the customer, it is necessary to *delight* or even *astonish* him or her. Fred Crawley (1993) admonished *"if quality was once a winning ticket, it is now no more than an admission ticket."*[31] For all companies in Nigeria, not only banks, this suggests that the sooner we got into the Quality train the less likelihood that we shall be left marooned in a wilderness of underdevelopment as the 21st century powers on.

Chapter Five

LEADERSHIP: THE KEY TO EXCELLENCE

"A leader rallies people to the future. You are a leader if, and only if, you are restless for change, impatient for progress, and deeply dissatisfied with the status quo."

Marcus Buckingham

The experience of companies and non-profit organizations that are implementing *Total Quality* show that strong leadership is the single most vital prerequisite for success on the journey. The importance of leadership in the Total Quality Management process is underscored by its being placed number one out of seven examination categories for the Malcolm Baldrige National Quality Award, the highest award for quality in the USA . The leadership category in the MBNQA has four sub categories viz: Senior Executive Leadership, Quality Values, Management for Quality and Public Responsiveness

The leadership category examines how the senior executive create and sustain a clear and visible Quality Value System along with a supporting management system to guide all activities of the company towards quality excellence. Also examined are the senior executives and the company's Quality leadership in the external community and how the company integrates its public responsiveness with its quality values and practices.

It is difficult to define leadership but Warren Bennis (1981) said, like beauty it is easy to recognize good leadership when you see one. Having tried for many years to define leadership without much success, Bennis settled for the following:
- the leader is the original, the manager is the copy
- the leader develops, the manager maintains.
- The leader originates, the manager imitates.
- The leader focuses on people, the manager focuses on systems
- The leader challenges status quo, the manager accepts it.
- The leader does the right thing, the manager does things right.[1]

Leadership as Steven Covey et al (1989, 1994), has observed is not management. Leadership is the *first creation*, while management is the *second creation*.[2] It is the leader's duty to create shared vision, strengthen, coach, and mentor to help develop the capabilities of individuals and the teams. It is the leader's duty to buid relationships of trust, do long-range planning, scan horizons, look at stock holders need, study the trends of the market, work on systems, create alignment. The leadership is the organ that spends time doing important things that makes the significant difference.[3]

Prominent business writers including Steven Covey, Tom Peters and Robert H. Waterman Jr. now believe that the leader has three key responsibilities:

1. Creating an empowering shared vision.
2. Articulating the business mission.
3. Cultivating shared values.

According to Steven Covey, vision is the ability to see beyond our present reality, to create, to invent what does not exist, to become what we not yet are. Vision affects the choices that we make. It is fueled by the realisation of the unique contribution we have the capacity to make - the legacy we can leave. It clarifies purpose, gives direction, and empowers us to perform beyond our resources. Shared vision becomes the constitution, the criterion for decision making in the group. It bonds people together. It gives them sense of unity and purpose that provide great strength in times of challenge.[4]

Steven Covey sees the mission as the blueprint before construction; the mental before the physical creation. An empowering mission statement gives meaningful expression to conscience inspired vision and values. Empowering mission statement focuses on contribution, on worthwhile purpose that create a collective deep burning "yes"! They come from the hearts and minds of everyone involved - not as *"an executive decree from Mount Olympus."* Empowering organizational mission statement are, as Steven Covey says, in harmony with what has come to be called universal mission *"to improve the economic well-being and quality of life of all stakeholders"*. Values are the supporting principles that guide the vision unto a successful fulfillment. Values motivate and sustain performance. They guide future actions and give the organization a reference point by which to examine past practices.[5]

Strong leadership is the sine quo non for successful implementation of Total Quality. As John Marous, then of Wettinghouse Coporation once said, implementing TQM requires *"strong emotional commitment at a very personal level from the chief executive"*. The Wallace Coporation in Texas, which won the Malcolm Baldridge National Quality Award in 1990 stated in the condensed version of the company's application for the Award *"....we know that 'leadership' means working closely with all employees, endorsing pride of workmanship, listening to and responing to suggestions of those closest to the job, focusing performance on the positive and developing team spirit. We are in a partnership of excellence in our business relationships, we accept tomorrow's challenge".*[6]

In her *In Search of Quality*, Sue McKibbin. Ph.D. (1990), postulated the following quality leadership action steps,[7] which no doubt captures in a nutshell what the leader needs to do as the organisation sets forth on the quality journey.

Be a Role Model: Reinforce your company's vision and goals through words and deeds. Remember that associates look to senior management for inspiration, strategic direction and sense of purpose. Articulate a quality-based vision for the company, then back it up with your actions.

Live Quality: Make quality your number one preoccupation. Think and talk quality day in and day out. Whenever there is a choice to be made, ask *"what's the best way to assure quality on this?"* No compromise or shortcuts are allowed. Ever! Even if they save time and money on the short term, they'll come back to haunt you later.

Communicate: Encourage two way communication. Listen to everyone, all the time. Ask questions and encourage honest answers. By keeping your finger in the pulse of the company, you'll be able to quickly spot problems and anticipate opportunities for quality improvement.

Remain Flexible: It may seem more natural to keep things predictable and controlled. But that usually gets in the way of productivity and customer satisfaction. Stay flexible, even if it feels uncomfortable at times.

Facilitate Employee Involvement: Delegate responsibilities, then step aside. Empower associates throughout your organization - not just those in management positions. Remember that everyone want to do their best and make significant contributions. Turn that desire into reality.

Reward Competence with Increased Authority: Encourage decision making at all levels by informed, competent individuals and teams. As a leader, consider being less decisive but more supportive. Refrain from second-guessing the work of others.

Find Errors in The System: Don't blame others if something goes wrong – that's the surest way to stifle initiative and squelch motivation. Instead of pointing fingers at people, identify process improvement alternatives so the mistake doesn't happen again.

Coach, Don't Boss: Don't be surprised if you do a little back sliding. It's perfectly normal to slip back into *"let me tell you what to do"* mode. When this happens, just shift gears. Remember, your job is to coach and support - not to boss.

Show That You Care: Make trust, respect and caring your own personal quality benchmarks. Without these three lynch pins, there can be no gains in your company's overall quality. Treat people inside and outside the company this way, and you will be well rewarded.

Chapter Six

NAILING THE BANKS: THE METHODOLOGY

*"The General desirous of winning a battle makes
many calculations in his temple beforehand"*

Sun Tsu (Chinese General), 500 BC

John A. Martilla and John C. James (1977) posited that services can be usefully rated according to their *customer importance* and *company performance*.[1] Measuring service elements according to their **"importance"** and **"performance"**, according to Martilla tells managers where to focus their efforts. Our study aimed to uncover the **"importance"** customers attach to certain service attributes or elements which together have been found to contribute to perceived quality of service in the banking industry, and how the subject banks were actually **"performing"** as regards these service attributes as adjudged by their customers in the Nigerian environment.

In the study we used the mall intercept survey method, with the questionnaire being our main survey instrument. We used two sets of questionnaires, and each questionnaire carried 14 similar service attributes questions. The first questionnaire tested attributes' **"customer importance"** while the second tested **"bank performance"**. The questionnaires were adapted from William B. Martin: **Managing Quality Customer Service** (1989),[2] and Laura A. Liswood: **Serving Them Right** (1991).[3] The attributes themselves (*determinants of service quality*) were originally developed by A. Parasuraman, Valerie A. Zeithaml, and Leonard L. Berry in their **"A Conceptual Model of Service Quality and its Implication for Future Research**, Journal of Marketing, Fall 1985, pp 4, and reproduced in Philip Kotler (1988), **Marketing Management: Analysis, Planning, Implementation, and Control**, 6th ed., Prentice Hall of India Private Ltd., New Delhi, pp 486.[4]

Customer Importance was rated on a four point scale of **"Extremely Important"**, **"Important"**, **"Slightly Important"**, and **"Not Important"**. The scores were then arrayed on intervals of 100 – 76 per cent (for **"extremely important"**) 75 – 51 per cent (for **"important"**), 50 – 26 per cent (for **"slightly important"**) and 25 – 0 per cent (for **"not important"**). Bank performance was similarly rated on a four point scale of **"Excellent"**, **"Good"**, **"Fair"** and **"Poor"**. The scores were similarly arrayed on intervals of 100 – 76 per cent (for **"excellent"**), 75 – 51 per cent (for **"good"**), 50 – 26 per cent (for **"fair"**) and 25 – 0 per cent (for **"poor"**). A total of 104 repondents comprising personal current account customers of the three banks were served the questionnaires by hand over a two-week period in Lagos and Kaduna, arguably the two most cosmopolitan cities in Nigeria.

For both "importance" and "performance", the rating intervals were:

Importance	Extremely Important	Important	Slightly Important	Not Important
Performance	(Excellent)	(Good)	(Fair)	(Poor)
	100-76%	75-51%	50-26%	25-0%

It was critical we determined whether there was any significant difference in the performance of the banks, and if so, which one was performing better. To determine the performance of the banks, analysis of the variance **(ANOVA)** was carried out using 5 per cent level of significance ($p < 0.05$). To pin point which bank was performing better, we used coefficient of variation. The data was analysed both manually and with SPSS (Statistical Package for Social Sciences) software at the Nigerian Institute for Trypanosomiasis Research (NITR), Kaduna.

In rating the performance of the banks, the hypothesis we tested were:

- Is there any significant difference in the performance of the banks? Use ANOVA. If yes, carry out multiple tests using *t*-test.
- If there is no significant difference, is there any evidence of one bank performing better than the other(s) – use coefficient of variation.

Before we look at the result of our findings in chapter seven, we herein give a brief historical background of the banking industry in Nigeria with emphasis on the then BIG THREE.

HISTORY OF BANK DEVELOPMENT IN NIGERIA

The history of the development of the banking system in Nigeria has been well documented by scholars such as Professor Green O. Nwankwo and others. Femi Adekanye, the founder and CEO of the defunct Commerce Bank Limited and a one time President of the Chartered Institute of Bankers of Nigeria (CIBN) is amongst the practitioners that have written on the subject. See his book, *The Elements of Banking in Nigeria* (1986, pp 167 – 169).[5]

The first commercial bank – the African Banking Corporation – opened its first branch in Lagos in 1892. Messrs. Elder Dempster & Co., a shipping firm based in Liverpool, England, was instrumental to its formation. The bank experienced some initial difficulties and eventually decided to transfer its interest fully to Elder Dempster & Co. in 1893. This led to the formation of a new bank known as the British Bank of West Africa (BBWA) in 1893 with £10,000 capital, later increased to £100,000 in the same year. It was registered in London as a limited liability company in March 1894 and the first Lagos Branch was opened that same year. Other branches were opened in major West African cities like Accra, Freetown and

Bathurst (present day Banjul, Gambia). The bank opened its second brance in Old Calabar in 1900

Another bank called the Anglo-African Bank was established in 1899 in Old Calabar by the Royal Niger Company (now UAC) to compete with BBWA. The bank later changed its name to Bank of Nigeria and established branches in Burutu, Lokoja and Jebba which were thriving commercial inland ports along the Niger River. However, due to fierce competition and the monopoly for the importation of silver from the Royal Mint enjoyed by BBWA, they sold out to BBWA, now First Bank, in 1912.

The second bank to establish a presence in Nigeria was Barclays Bank DCO (Dominion, Colonial and Overseas). Its first branch was opened in Lagos in 1917. Soon after, nine other brances were opened in different parts of the country. Following the indeginisation decree of 1968 Barclays became Union Bank of Nigeria Ltd. (now Plc.)

The third commercial bank with expatriate connections to set up in Nigeria was the British and French Bank now called United Bank for Africa (UBA). The bank was established in 1949.

Together these three banks controlled close to 90 per cent of aggregate bank deposits up to the late eighties. From 1914 to early 1930, several abortive attempts were made to establish locally owned and managed banks to break the foreign monopoly.

The foreign banks came principally to render services in connection with international trade, so their relationships at that time were chiefly with the expatriate trading companies and with the government. They largely ignored the development of local African entrepreneurship.

Indigenous banks came into the scene around 1929 when the Industrial and Commercial Bank was set up by a group of Nigerians. The bank folded up in 1930 due to undercapitalisation, poor management and aggressive competition by the expatriate banks. In 1931 another indigenous bank, the Nigerian Merchant Bank was established. Like its predecessor, it went into liquidation in 1936. Earlier in 1933, a group of pioneers launched the National Bank of Nigeria Limited, which was the first Indigenous bank to survive. The next private indigenous bank to be established was the Agbonmagbe Bank, founded by Chief Okupe in 1945. The bank was taken over by the Western State Government in 1969 and its name changed to Wema Bank. The fifth bank, The Nigerian Penny Bank, set up in the early 1940s, collapsed in 1949 due to mismanagement. This was followed by Nigerian Farmers and Commercial Bank in 1947 which failed in 1953. The Merchants Bank was the next to open for business in 1952 but closed in 1960.

Between 1947 and 1952 a total of 22 banks were registered in Nigeria according to a study conducted by the Central

Bank of Nigeria. However, a figure as high as 185 banks was quoted from the government records and was confirmed by the Financial Secretary as the number actually registered as banking companies between 1947 and 1952, of which 145 were registered in 1947 and 40 in 1952. Most of these banks, however, merely registered without actually commencing operations. One of the more successful indigenous banks was the African Continental Bank (ACB) founded by Nnamdi Azikiwe in 1947.

The need for legislation for the control of banking in Nigeria became apparent, if only to protect depositors. The Colonial Governement therefore set up a commission of inquiry – the Paton Commission. Consequent upon the report of the Commission the first banking legislation was passed in 1952.

In spite of the enactment of the Banking Ordinance of 1952 banks were still indulging in some malpractices which the Act could not effectively control. Therefore, the necessity for establishing a Central Bank to supervise and control the banks became more apparent and pressing. Thus, the Central Bank of Nigeria came into being in 1959.

A new Banking Ordinance was promulgated in 1958. Through this Act, the conditions for establishing new banks were tightened and the capital requirements, especially for foreign banks, were doubled from the equivalent of N200,000 under the 1952 Act to N400,000. This was again increased to N1.5 million in 1969.

Up to the year 1984, there were only 35 commercial and merchant banks in the country but between 1985 and 1992 there was an explosion in bank numbers brought about by the deregulation of the financial system by the General Ibrahim Babangida administration. By 1992 the number of merchant banks and commercial banks in the country had climbed to 115. However, by 1995 about 5 commercial and merchant banks had been wound up. As at the time of this project (December 1995) many banks were in distress condition and were in the process of merging with one another while many others were under direct supervision of the Central Bank of Nigeria (CBN) and Nigerian Deposit Insurance Corporation (NDIC).

The major legislations regulating the practice of banking in the country as at the time of our research were, the Central Bank of Nigeria Decree (Decree No 24) of 1991, Banks and Other Financial Institutions Decree (BOFID) (Decree No. 25) of 1991, and the Failed Banks (Recovery of Debts) And Financial Malpractises in Banks (Decree No. 18) of 1994. Following the restoration of democratic governance, these decrees were amended to Acts of the National Assembly.

THE BIG THREE

First Bank of Nigeria Plc.
First Bank prepared the following profile in 1994 as part of their Centenary Celebration. It was reproduced in the nineth edition of **Nigerian Banking, Finance, and Commerce**, a publication

of Research and Data Services Limited (REDASEL), page 73.[6]

First Bank of Nigeria Plc. is the pioneer and premier banking institution in Nigeria. The bank has its origins in a British Bank, African Banking Corporation (ABC) which established a branch in Lagos in 1892 through the effort of Sir Alfred Lewis Jones, the Chairman of Elder Dempster and Co. and Mr. George Beville, the Company's agent in Lagos.

In 1893, the branch was acquired by Elder Dempster and Co. and on March 31, 1894, the Bank of British West Africa (BBWA) was registered as a limited liability company with Sir Alfred Jones as the founding Chairman.

It commenced business at its head office in Liverpool England with a paid up Capital if £12,000. Its Lagos office (at Marina) was opened on May 1894 and since then, the Bank has grown to a formidable size weathering great and turbulent economic storms of both the pre and the post independent Nigeria. Today, the bank has become the most captivating story in the banking community with a hundred years of banking services to the nation. In 1896, a branch office of BBWA was opened in Accra, Gold Coast (now Ghana). Another was established in Freetown, Sierra Leone in 1898, and in 1902 a branch was also sited in Bathurst (Gambia).

The second branch in Nigeria was opened in Calabar in 1907 and a few years later services had extended to the Northern part of Nigeria with the opening of Zaria branch in 1912. Also in 1912, BBWA further demonstrated its growth intentions by absorbing another bank, the Anglo African Bank (AAB), later Bank of Nigeria, established in 1899.

It was later renamed Bank of West Africa (BWA) in 1957 to reflect the new independence status of West African countries served by the bank. Again in 1966, the Bank of West Africa merged with Standard Chartered Bank, resulting in a change in the name to Standard Bank of West Africa.

Follwing the promulgation of the Companies Decree of 1968 and the Banking Decree of 1969, the bank was incorporated locally and renamed Standard Bank of Nigeria Limited. In 1972, Standard Chartered Bank gradually began to reduce its shareholding from 60 per cent to 40 per cent in line with the provision of the indigenisation Decree. As at the time of the project, Standard Chartered Bank had 38 per cent of the total equity.

In order to reflect its Nigerian majority shareholding, and to underscore its pioneering status in the field of modern competitive banking, the name was changed to First Bank of Nigeria Limited in 1979 and First Bank of Nigeria Plc. in 1992. In the same year, the Federal Military Government sold its equity participation of 48.2 per cent. Thus, the shareholding of the First bank of Nigeria stood at 62 per cent Nigerian and 38 per cent Standard Chartered Bank as at the 1995. However, at the time of the report, Standard Chartered Bank Africa Plc.

was in the process of reducing its shareholding from 38 per cent to 9.9 per cent.

As at the the time of our project, First Bank had the largest network of branches in the financial system with 287 branches located in thirty states including the Federal Capital Territory, Abuja. Through the branches, the Bank provides a comprehensive range of commercial banking services geared towards the continuing development of the nation's economy.

At the onset, the Bank concentrated on financing agricultural export and general commerce. With developments in the economy, the mass market orientation was complemented with development of skills and capabilities to service the corporate customer segment of the market. Today, First Bank offers services to cater for customers needs across the broad spectrum of the market from retail to commercial, corporate and international customers. The Bank indeed sees itself not merely as a provider of banking services but renders financial services to other related financial institutions.

The services provided by the bank can be broadly classified as follows: deposit collection, fund transmission, foreign currency, credit, financial services, development banking services, and export services.

The bank had record performance in 1992 and 1993. The results clearly confirm the Bank's leadership position in the industry, a fact conferred on it by history and by performance.

Gross earnings for the year 1993 increased by 60.2 per cent from N2.689 billion to N4.309 billion while profit betore tax at N931.8 million was N565.8 million or 154.6 per cent higher than the N366 million recored in 1992. The bank's after tax profit was N584.5 million compared to N334.7 million achieved in 1992, i.e. a growth of 75 per cent. At half year 1993, the bank paid an interim dividend of 20k per share. A final dividend of 50k per share and a bonus issue of one new share for every one held were declared at the Annual General Meeting held in April, 1994.

Total deposit of the bank increased by over 40 per cent from N11.9 billion in 1992 to N16.4 billion in 1993. Total assets grew by 38.8 per cent to N23.6 billion from N17 billion. Share holders' funds rose by 56.9 per cent to N1.5 billion, while the capital adequacy in accordance with the basic computation stands at 15.76 per cent as against 8 per cent recommended by the regulatory authorities.

What is more important to the bank, even beyond the impressive operating performance is its approach to business reflected in commitment to operating within the regulatory framework and with high level of intergrity in the art of banking and ample regard to its social responsibilities. This approach and commitment are vividly captured in our mission statement.

"The mission of the First Bank of Nigeria Plc is historically determined. Its primary objective must be to remain true to its name at all times as the leading financial institution in the

*country by providing to its customers across the nation and
beyond, within the parameters of regulatory policies, the best
banking services available."[7]*

UNION BANK OF NIGERIA PLC

As was pointed out earlier Union Bank of Nigeria Plc. was the
second foreign bank to establish a presence in Nigeria, then
as Barclays Bank DCO (Dominion, Colonial and Overseas).
Its first branch was opened in Lagos in 1917. Soon after, nine
other branches were opened in different parts of the country.
The bank maintained a strong link with its overseas parents,
Barclays Bank Plc. until 1968 when following the indeginisation
decree it became Union Bank of Nigeria Ltd.

Today the bank has set an impressive record in the industry.
By September 1994, the bank had altogether 255 branches
including off shore ones and had a staff strength of 12,325.[8]
Tha bank today is 100 per cent Nigerian owned, Barclays Bank
Plc. having divested its interest in the bank. With total assets
of N43.51 billion and deposit of N28.03 bilion as at 1994, the
bank was easily the largest bank in Nigeria by assest, even
though it had 32 less branches than its arch rival, First Bank.

The bank provides full range of financial services including
deposit collection, fund transmission, foreign currency, credit,
financial services, development banking services and export
services. It has recently set up subsidiaries to compete in

such areas as mortgage financial services, and discount house services. As at 1993 the bank had won the Nigerian Stock Exchange Presidents Award nine times out of a total of 17 since the inception of the Award. It was also adjudged the Best Bank under Agricultural Credit Gurantee Scheme Fund (ACGSF) in 1993, thus becoming the first bank to win the prestigious award. If this was the story circa 1995, today the story is sadly different.

UNITED BANK OF AFRICA PLC

The United Bank of Africa Plc. (UBA) is one of Nigeria's top three commercial banks. It was established in 1961 by a consortium of 5 international banks to take over the banking business carried on in Nigeria since 1949 by the British and French Bank Limited. With assets of N24 billion and 199 branches spread all over Nigeria the Bank has recorded an impressive growth rate.[9] UBA is active in all aspects of commercial banking and provides international banking, trusteeship, share registration, corporate finance services through specialized divisions and subsidiaries.

An aggressive business promotion strategy coupled with a willingness to innovate has earned the bank enviable position in the banking industry. UBA Plc. is strongly committed to its social responsibilities and identifies with the communities in which it is represented. Nigerian interest constitutes 60 per cent of the shareholding of the bank. Four of the founding international banks namely, Banque National de Paris, Bankers International Corporation, New York, Banca Nazional del Lavoro, and Monte dei Paschi di Siena, which altogether own 40 per cent of the shareholding are still represented on the Board of Directors and continue to make their expertise and resources throughout the world available to assist the bank and its customers. UBA Plc. has branches in New York and Grand Cayman Island and a Representative Office in London. It also maintains correspondent relationship with many banks in Africa and in major countries in the world.

If the above stories were the positions of the troika, as the then were, in 1995, today the situation is altogether different, with Union in a titanic battle for survival while its former arch rivals, First Bank and UBA power on. UBA Plc. has since changed its strategy and now pursues pan-African ambition to become Africa's global bank, and now has subsidiaries in 19 African countries as at the last count, with Congo (DCR) being the latest. The total assets of the bank closed at N1.54trillion as at December 31, 2009, the latest year figures are available.[10] No doubt the figure is too stale to be taken seriously but the bank has made its intenstions known – Africa's Global Bank.

Meanwhile, First Bank's total assets closed at N1.95trillion as at December 31, 2010. To "consolidate its position", First Bank has embarked on *total transformation"* to become what it calls "the undisputed leader".[11] Sadly, the financials of Union Bank post CBN's intervention remain a closely guarded secret. A search at http://www.unionbankng.com/history.htm on May

15, 2011 did not yield much, except that as at March 31, 2009, about two months before the CBN's hammer descended, the bank had 405 branches and total assets of N1.10trillion.[12] It's clear that the *Stallion* is no longer *''Big, Strong and Reliable"* as it once was.

Chapter Seven

THE FALL FROM GRACE: HOW UNION FAILED THE EXCELLENCE TEST

"Competing in the marketplace is like war, you have injuries and casualties, and the best strategy wins."

JOHN C. COLLINS

ANALYSIS OF ATTRIBUTES IMPORTANCE

Analysis of the data revealed that customers attach **high importance** to all the attributes under study. The mean importance rating ranged between 96 per cent and 66 per cent, meaning the attributes were all regarded either as **"extremely important"** or **"important"**. From the data, we infer that the three major testers of *Quality* in the Nigerian banking environment are as at the time of the study were:

- The speed at which customers are served.
- Accuracy of information about transactions.
- Availability of equipments to work with.

The speed at which customers are served relates to productivity as expressed by the number of customers served per unit of time. Improvement of the speed of services represents an important opportunity that a bank can exploit to keep its customers satisfied, and an important competitive edge. The new generation banks were already exploiting this competitive edge to their advantage, while THE BIG THREE at the time still took speed for granted as their services were not *computerised,* as was the lexicon then.

Accuracy of information about transactions with the bank is first and foremost about trustworthiness, character, intergrity, credibility and reliability of the institution. The whole essence of banking is about trust. When there is threat to the intergrity of a financial institution, it loses its credibility as a safe and sensible place to transact business. Once that credibility is lost, the institution becomes suspect and is likely to suffer over time a fatal loss of business. This is why banks should not gloss over the bases they calculate fees, charges and the interest rate on customers' accounts. The more open or transparent a financial institution is about transactions with its customers, the better and the higher its reputation in the eyes of the public. The method of calculation should be made as simple as it possibly can.

In descending order of importance, the attributes were rated as shown in the table below.

Table 7.1: All The Attributes - In Descending Order of Importance[*]

Attributes	Attribute Description	Mean Importance Rating %
1	Promptness of Service	96.23
3	Accuracy of Information	92.13
12	Availability of Equipments	90.45
4	Clarity of Account Statements	88.64
9	Availability of Information	87.48
11	Nice Working Environment	85.65
2	Professionalism of Staff	85.19
7	Reputation of Bank	84.54
10	Convenient Hours of Operation	81.13
5	Courtesy of Staff	79.25
13	Generally Welcoming	78.24
6	Knowledge of Staff	68.87
14	Say Thank You	67.73
8	Friendliness of Staff	66.36

[*] See Appendix 3 for a fuller description of the attributes and the order they appeared in our study.

What determines or directly influences speed of services is the **"availability of equipments to work with"**. These include computers, cash counting machines, scanners, fax machines, photocopiers, to mention but a few. Absence of equipments greatly compromises speed as was the case with the Big Three then. For instance, of the three banks under study, only First Bank had computers in its front office to service its current account customers in its Yakubu Gowon Way (then Hospital Road) branch in Kaduna.

A close look at the attributes reveals that 11 of the 14 attributes have to do with structure, policy and procedure areas, usually under the purview of management. As is well known, only management can initiate the move towards *Quality Customer Service*. This move usually involves realigning structures and changing policies all aimed at facilitating customer care.

Areas which staff have direct influence and which they can do something about are the areas where they have direct contact with customers and this can be changed through attitude training and indoctrination, much more faster than changing structures and policies. The three attributes under this heading are **"Courtesy of Staff"**, **"Friendliness of Staff"**, and **"Say Thank You"**. Ultimately, the key lies in staff recruitment and selection. Frontline people must be people with passion for the customer: friendly, approachable, with smiles constantly on their faces. Grouches have no place on the frontlines.

Jack Welch, the former CEO of GE, emphasized in his book, **Winning**. *"Hiring great people is brutally hard"*, 'and yet nothing matters more in winning than getting the right people on the field.'*[1]* As Welch admonished, all the strategic plans and super computers are worthless if you don't have the right men and women in place. Management expert and co-author of **The One Minute Manager**, Ken Blanchard, recounts in his latest Book, **The Secret**, co-authored with Mark Miller, former Vice

President, Training and Development, Chick-fil-A, Inc., that Peter Drucker, was once asked, *"What is the most important decision an executive makes?"* Drucker replied, *"Who does what?"* Getting the right people in the right jobs is the most important job of the leader, it cannot be delegated to the HR or HCM unit. To manage people well, Welch postulates the following company-wide practices, amongst others, *"Elevate HR to a position of power and primacy in the organization, and make sure HR people have the special qualities to help managers build leaders and careers."*[2] Welch said the best HR people came across as *"pastors and parents"*[3] rolled into one.

ANALYSIS OF THE BANKS PERFORMANCE

In analysing the performance, we compared the banks' performance on each attribute with the importance customers attached to the attributes, and compared also how the banks rated among themselves. Arising from this, we made deductions about the banks' attitude to quality customer service, and established which bank was better overall. Importance - Performance Matrix (See Figure 7.1 further below) shows in graphic detail where the banks fell short.

The banks' performance was rated as being **"good"** in 13 attributes and **"fair"** in one attribute. The banks did not achieve **"excellent"** in any attribute, as shown in the table below.

Table 7.2   BANKS PERFORMANCE

Attribute (Assigned No)	Attribute Description	Banks Performance Mean Rating %
1	Promptness of service	55.71
2	Professionalism of staff	65.29
3	Accuracy of information	69.15
4	Clarity of account statement	67.97
5	Courtesy of staff	53.17
6	Knowledge of staff	62,38
7	Reputation of bank	58.96
8	Friendliness of staff	55.14
9	Availability of information	61.47
10	Convenient hours of operation	67.81
11	Nice working environment	73.10
12	Availability of equipment	63.39
13	Generally welcoming	53.59
14	Say thank you	62.38

Details how the individual banks performed are highlighted in Appendix 1.

From the summary table below we observe that while customers regarded 11 of the attributes as **"extremely important"** and 3 as **"important"**, the banks performance was merely **"good"** in all except one attribute. How the banks measured up can best be captured by putting the **"importance"** and **"performance"** ratings side by side as shown in the table. As earlier highlighted, the banks were not **"excellent"** in any attribute, but were **"good"** in 13 and **"fair"** in one. Being "good" can be dangerous as we will soon find out.

Table 7.3: Banks Rating:Attribute Importance vs Banks Performance

Attributes Importance	Extremely Important	Important	Slightly Important	Not Important
(Banks Performance)	(Excellent)	(Good)	(Fair)	(Poor)
Importance	11	3	Nil	Nil
(Performance)	(Nil)	(13)	(1)	Nil

GAP ANALYSIS

The gap between what customers judged as **"important"** and the banks **"performance"** on the surveyed attributes is given in table 7.4., below.

From analysis of the data, we observed that the banks overall performed *indifferently*, meaning they were neither "excellent" nor "poor" in the attributes relative to the importance customers attached to the attributes. In all cases, the **"mean performance rating"** were below the **"mean importance rating"** as highlighted in table 7.4.

We can pin point where the banks particularly failed short of customers' expectations by looking at the Gap, that is the difference between the Mean Importance Rating and the Mean Performance Rating.

Table 7.4   IMPORTANCE VERSUS PERFORMANCE GAP (ALL BANKS)

Attributes (Number Assigned)	Attribute Description	Atrribute Importance Mean Rating (%)	Banks Performance Mean Rating (%)	Banks Performance GAP (%)
1	Promptness of service	96.23	55.71	40.52
3	Accuracy of information	92.13	69.15	22.98
12	Availability of equipments	90.45	63.39	27.06
4	Clarity of account statements	88.64	67.97	20.67
9	Availability of information	87.48	61.47	25.81
11	Nice working environment	85.65	73.10	12.55
2	Professionalism of Staff	85.19	65.29	19.90
7	Reputation of bank	84.54	58.96	25.58
10	Convenient hours of operation	81.13	67.81	13.32
5	Courtesy of staff	79.25	53.17	26.08
13	Generally welcoming	78.24	53.59	24.65
6	Knowledge of Staff	68.87	62.38	6.49
14	Say Thank you	67.73	44.69	23.04
8	Friendliness of Staff	66.36	55.14	11.22

To reduce customers' pain points, the subject banks must work to narrow the gaps to avoid customers backlash, for example, by reduced patronage as Union Bank is experiencing.

By working hard to narrow the gap, customers' satisfaction can be improved. By order of performance gap, the most important attributes the banks need to work on for immediate pay off are highlighted in table 7.5 below.

Table 7.5   CRITICAL ATTRIBUTES TO FOCUS EFFORT (ALL BANKS)

Attribute Description	Attribute Importance Mean Rating (%)	Banks Performance Mean Rating (%)	Banks Performance Gap (%)
Promptness to service	96-23	55.71	40.52
Availability of Equipments	90.45	63.39	27.06
Courtesy of Staff	79.25	53.17	26.08

The gaps represent both opportunity and challenge. Narrowing the gap by any significant margin can give an immediate pay off. What the gaps mean in reality is that, as organisations, the banks should be outward looking, that is, they should listen more to their customers. As Peter Drucker points out *"… to the customer, no product or service, and certainly no company, is of much importance. All he is interested in are his own values, his own wants, his own reality. For this reason alone, any serious attempt to state 'what our business is' must start with the customer, his realities, his situation, his behaviour, his expectations, and his values."*[4]

The banks scored relatively high (73 per cent) in *"Nice Working Enviroment and Physical Layout"*, with UBA taking the lead. This attribute was rated 6th by customers in order of importance, with a score of 85.65 per cent. All the same this means the banks still have a long way to go in meeting customers expectations as far as this attribute is concerned as the score was 12.55. percentage points below customers' importance rating of the attribute. For instance the banks at the time had no comfortable seats in some of their branches, while in some branches the air conditioning systems were not functioning properly leaving their banking halls stuffy and uncomfortable. The poor working environment no doubt negatively affected staff and invariably their attitude towards customers.

Looking again at the gaps, the least in the array was 6.49 per cent for **"Knowledge of Staff"**. This means that staff *technical knowledge* and customer expectation, as far as this attributes is concerned, is not very different, and the banks would not need to worry much in this direction. However, a quick look at the attributes, "**Courtesy of staff**", "**Say thank you**", and **"Friendliness"**, with gaps of 26.08 per cent, 23.04 per cent and 11.22 per cent respectively confirms to us that, in deliverying Quality Customers Service, technical competence alone is not enough. The people dimension must be correct. As far as **"Knowledge of Staff"** is concerned, we must not lose sight of the fact that the banks employ from the same "pool of knowledge", the employees attended the same universities, polytechnics and secondary schools, hence the low gap. While knowledge may be the same, it's the organisational culture that has the biggest impact on the way staff see their duty to the customer.

The three attributes *courtesy, say thank you* and *friendliness* have to do with attitude towards the job, and attitude toward the customer. Attitude training and motivating staff for empathetic approach towards the customer, and equipping them with the right equipment to do the job, are therefore the key to providing *Quality Customer Service*.

Overall the performance indicated that for the 'BIG THREE', the journey to excellence had not yet begun and customers were not getting value for their patronage. As the three banks accounted for about 70 per cent of the total deposit turnover of the commercial banking industry, they were supposed to take the lead in dictating the pace of change, innovation, entrepreneurship and customer care in the industry. From the analysis, at least as far as customer care was concerned, we saw that as at the time, that was not the case. As we commented then, unless the indifferent attitude towards *Quality* Customer Service changes, the future of the industry will remain bleak. Sadly for Union Bank it has stubbed its feet as we feared then and the Gods of Quality had no choice but to exact justice.

IMPORTANCE - PERFORMANCE MATRIX

Another way of looking at the ratings is to plot the Mean Importance and Mean Performance Ratings on a four - dimensional matrix to observe the cluster of the attributes relative to the matrix. The relative location of an attributes on the matrix directs management's attention to where to focus effort. The aim is to reach the upper right hand corner of quadrant B. The measure of the distance from the location of an attribute in the matrix space to the upper right hand corner indicates the amount of effort management need to expend to achieve excellence.

The figure below shows the relative location of the attributes *mean*s on the Importance - Performance Matrix, for the three banks combined. The matrix (figure 7.1) shows that three services attributes ("**Knowledge of Staff**", "**Friendliness of Staff**", and "**Say Thank You**") are regarded as **"Important"**, while the rest are regarded as **"Extremely Important"**. However the figure also tells us that the banks were not performing any in an **"Excellent"** manner. The service attribute (number 14), "**Say Thank You**", in quadrant A is the least well performed and management's effort is required to move to quadrant B. However, in focusing effort, management must apply the Pareto principle, by also analysing the gap, to establish where effort will yield the highest payoff.

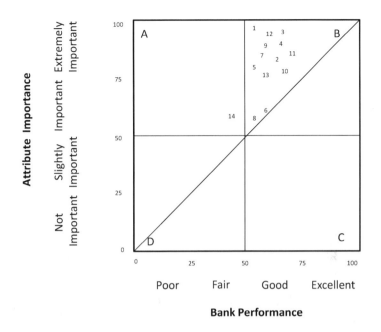

Figure 7.1: Importance – Performance Matrix Indicating
The Relative Position of Attributes In The Matrix Space

In this regard the highest pay off will be achieved by focusing on "promptness of service", "availability of equipment", and "courtesy of staff", as we have already highlighted. In all cases, the aim is to increase service performance level to match customers' expectations. Where this is not possible, effort should be made to lower customers' expectations through dialogue and not by pretending the problems (pain points) do not exist. In all cases the aim is to reach the extreme right hand corner in quadrant B. The Mean Performance Rating of excellent companies cluster around the extreme right hand corner in quadrant B. As we earlier pointed out, measuring service elements according to their *Importance* and *Performance* tells managers where to focus their efforts.

INDIVIDUAL BANK PERFORMANCE

With regard to the individual banks, ANOVA was carried out to find out whether there was any significant difference in their performance. Below is the result obtained from the analysis.

Source	Df	SS	MS	F	P
Factor	2	0.4160	0.2080	7.88	0.001
Error	39	1.0290	0.0264		
Total	41	1.4450			

$p < 0.05$

Where:

P Value: -   Probability of rejecting or accepting the null hypothesis

under   a   particular   level   of significance (5%)

Ho : μ -   Performance does not differ (null hypothesis).

Ha : μ -   Performance differ (alternative hypothesis)

Df   -   Degree of freedom

SS   -   Sum of Square

MS   -   Mean Square

F   -   Test statistic

p   -   Probability

If $P < 0.05$, reject Ho or otherwise accept Ho. Since P – value is small, there is enough evidence based on the data to reject Ho. The banks performed differently.

To establish which of the three banks performed better multiple t-tests were carried out. The following results were obtained:

1. C1 = FBN, C2 = UBN
Diff. N=14, Mean = 0.2307, S = 0.1078, T = 8.01, P = 0.000
$p < 0.05$

2. C1 = FBN, C2 = UBA
Diff. N = 14, Mean = 0.1836, S = 0.1213, T = 5.66, P = 0.0001
$p < 0.05$

3. C1 = UBN, C2 = UBA
Diff. N = 14, Mean = -0.0471, S = 0.0858, T = 2.06, P = 0.97
$p > 0.05$

Where:
T = test statistic
S = standard deviation

The above test shows that FBN performed better that UBN and UBA, while UBN and UBA performed somewhat the same way. Accordingly it can be inferred that FBN induced the difference in the analysis of the variance result. Df = 2.

To further pin-point the difference in the performance of the banks, particularly between UBN and UBA, the coefficient of variation of performance of the banks was analysed. Below is the data we obtained:

	FBN	UBN	UBA
$\overline{\overline{X}}$	67.99	56.41	58.77
S^2	24.40	80.73	96.01
$\overline{S}$	4.94	8.99	9.79
CV, %	7.67	15.94	10.20

Where:

$\overline{\overline{X}}$ -   The mean of the means.

S^2 -   Variance of the sample.

$\overline{S}$ -   Standard error of the mean.

CV, %   -   Coefficient of variation.

The coefficient of variation confirm that FBN performed better than UBN and UBA (FBN = 7.67%, UBN = 15.94, UBA = 10.20%). Even though the multiple tests and analysis of variance did not reveal any significant difference between UBN and UBA, there is enough evidence to conclude that UBA performed better than UBN; from the coefficient of variation (UBN = 15.94%, UBA = 10.20%). See Appendix 7.2 for formula used for the calculations.

That UBN should perform worst than the others was not totally unexpected. In most cases the staff of UBN said their corporate strategy was to focus on corporate customers (whatever that means). In a particular instance during the survey, a potential customer about to open an account approached a staff of UBN for an explanation on how to complete the account opening form and the staff retorted it was not her duty. Such instances were not isolated but this particular occurrence at the Hospital Road (now Yakubu Gowon Way), Kaduna branch of Union Bank was the most poignant. Small episodes such as the one highlighted above no doubt added up to turn the table against Union Bank, and the Gods of Quality being no respecter of persons or institutions that defile the hallowed chambers of excellence had no choice but to strike back.

Epilogue

"...it's not the big that eat the small, it's the fast that eat the slow."

Laurence Houghton

*"Don't be encumbered by history.
Go out and create something wonderful."*

Robert Noyce

Without Mallam Sanusi Lamido Sanusi's coup de grace perhaps Union Bank and the other ailing banks would have been carrying on business as usual, winning all sorts of awards along the way. It is for this reason that we dedicate this book to the CBN Governor for his uncommon courage and single minded pursuit of sanitisation of the banking industry. If the plans to recapitalise the rescued banks succeed, Union Bank like phoenix, may indeed rise from the ashes of disgrace and begin a new lease on life, but the banking landscape will never be the same again as the Zeniths and GTBs of this world will not stand still.

True, the UBA and First Bank of yesterday that we studied are entirely different from the UBA and First Bank, and even Union Bank of today. Today we talk about the new UBA and the new FBN, where automation, customer delightment and laser-like focus on the market is the mantra. We have never doubted that the BIG THREE have all it takes to begin the journey to excellence. Infact, UBA's ATM network is now the standard in the industry, while those of most second tier banks without mentioning names are noted for down time especially on week ends. That having been said, UBA and FBN should not rest on their laurels for they still have a lot of catching up to do in terms of responsiveness, and overall staff attitude.

At the heart of apathy towards the customer is poor staff motivation and attitude training. In the very short run massive training, unlearning of the old ways, learning and relearning of new ways are required but in the long run the banks need a total culture change to become more outwardly focused towards the customers than what presently pertains. This struggle for the hearts and minds must be led by executive management of the banks. Bold leadership is called for.

According to Marcus Buckingham, *''A leader rallies people to the future. Leaders are fascinated by the future. You are a leader if, and only if, you are restless for change, impatient for progress, and deeply dissatisfied with the status quo.''*[1] *''As a leader''* he explains, *''you are never satisfied with the present, because in your head you can see a better future, and the friction between 'what is' and 'what could be' burns you, stirs you up, propels you forward. This is leadership.''*[2] Does the management of UBA and FBN have the leadership mojo, as Marshall Goldsmith would say, to take their respective banks to the next level? From their present actions I would say they have. FBN has embarked on total transformation, and in the mold of Bank of America that has the US as the bedrock of its competitive strategy, FBN has Nigeria as the centrepiece of its competitive strategy in its bid to confirm its "undisputed leadership". UBA on the other hand has adopted Citigroup's strategy of total global dominance, and guns for total pan-African dominance. Whatever strategy FBN and UBA adopt, one thing they should never forget is that it is all about the customer. PERIOD! Any bank, be it FBN, UBA, or any other bank for that matter that stakes a bold claim to unequivocally fly the QED (*Quality Every Day*) flag will win my vote of confidence any day.

Excellence in all its various dimensions (Personal Excellence, Corporate Excellence, Customer Excellence) is now regarded as one of the most important determinants of company performance and profitability in the corporate world. The Total Quality Movement started in Japan in the late 1950s cum early 1960s, and spread to the USA and western Europe in the late 1970s / early 1980s, and it is now being embraced the world over by organisations as diverse as manufacturing companies, service companies, government establishments, non-governmental organisations, and even governments. As Berry and others point out, *"customers expectations about levels of service are entirely reasonable."* Hold outs and all organisations, be they governmental or private that only pay lip service to quality or are simply unable to discern the changing world view will simply sink into irrelevance.

This Project studied the "**importance**" bank customer attach to 14 attributes that have been known to affect Quality

Customer Service delivery and how the erstwhile BIG THREE banks ranked in their "**performance**" in the attributes. Our study established that the banks were indifferent to *Quality* as none was positively **"excellent"** in their performance, but they were not outrightly **"poor"**. Sadly Union Bank, which came bottom in our ranking is now struggling for survival as we warned. Would the story have been different if Union Bank had heeded our warning? Will Union be spared by the GODS OF QUALITY? Quality may not be a cure-all medicine for all company's ills but without it you will surely die. Without quality you will be tempted to steal, cook your books, and defraud, but all those straws in the wind will not serve the interest of your customers, employees, and the society at large.

FBN and UBA, as the oldest banks, with the largest branch networks, deposits, and the asset bases, have the historically determined mandate to change the banking industry in Nigeria for the better, and in the process, tug the country on a trajectory of enlightened development. Single minded pursuit of profit, if anything, will be counter productive in the long run. Marvin Bower, the founder of Mckinsey & Co. was quoted as saying that *"the primary goals of a successful firm does not include profit. Generally this should be subordinated. If you do it well, the profits will come. Any service business that gives a higher priority to profit deserves to fail".*

If you think Quality or Excellence is all about hot air, let me ask you, are you happy staying in darkness? Why is PHCN unable to supply light? Everybody in this country should start asking the question: Why is there no light? Why is there no development in the local goverments? All companies and organisations, both public and private in this country must rise up and start operating under the quality tenets: the customer comes first. Let's all urgently embark, in words and in deed, on the journey to Excellence with the Customer as the centre of the universe in all that we do. We should all be concerned with the issues of Quality, the public sector not exempted: the presidency, national assembly, states assemblies, local government councils, government agencies and parastatals. You owe the citizens and your employees the duty to provide quality service. As Fred Crawley, the ex-Chairman Girobank, once said, *"if quality was once a winning ticket, it is now no more than an admission ticket."* While we are here talking about just the *basic* quality of goods and services, countries the worldover are already embarking on what is called level five *Quality*, otherwise expressed as *customer experience*. Unless we begin the journey today, we will continue to remain behind even in basic necessities such as electricity, water, and quality living. Look at our gutters! Look at our schools!! Look at poverty all over the place!!! It's clear, the sooner we got started the better. Quality is now the way of life. Let's Embrace it! Let's Live it!! Wishing you a Safe JOURNEY.

Appendix

Appendix 1

Individual Bank Performance Relative to Attribute Importance

Attribute Assigned Number	Attribute Description (Abridged)	FBN %	UBN %	UBA %	All Banks %	Attribute Importance %
1.	Promptness of Service	67.74	47.86	51.52	55.71	96.23
2.	Professionalism	70.16	59.43	65.29	64.96	85.19
3.	Accuracy of Information	77.42	64.58	65.44	69.15	92.13
4.	Clarity of Account	72.50	64.71	66.69	67.97	88.64
5.	Courtesy of Staff	60.94	49.31	49.26	53.17	79.25
6.	Knowledge of Staff	68.10	59.48	59.56	62.38	68.87
7.	Reputation of Bank	64.84	53.47	58.57	58.96	84.54
8.	Friendliness of Staff	64.84	52.78	47.79	55.14	66.36
9.	Availability of Information	67.95	53.57	62.88	61.47	87.48
10.	Convenient Hours of Operations	69.35	66.67	67.42	67.81	81.13
11.	Nice Working Environment	75.00	67.86	76.43	73.10	85,65
12.	Availability of Equipments	68.75	62.86	58.57	63.39	90.45
13.	Generally Welcoming	64.84	52.08	52.86	56.59	78.24
14	Say Thank You	59.5	35.29	39.29	44.69	67.73

Appendix 2

Formula Used For Calculating:

1. **Variance**

$$S^2 = \frac{\Sigma(Xi-\bar{X})^2}{N}$$

2. **Standard Deviation**

$$S = \frac{\Sigma(Xi-\bar{X})^2}{N}$$

3. **Coefficient of Variation**

$$V = \frac{\bar{S} \times 100}{\bar{\bar{X}}}$$

Where:

Xi—The observation value

$\bar{X}$—The mean of the observations.

$\bar{S}$—Standard error of the mean.

$\bar{\bar{X}}$—The mean of the means.

N—The number of observations

Derivation of Coefficient of Variation for the Three Banks

$$CV\ (FBN) = \frac{4.94 \times 100}{67.99} = 7.67\%$$

$$CV\ (UBN) = \frac{8.99 \times 100}{56.41} = 15.94\%$$

$$CV\ (UBA) = \frac{9.79 \times 100}{96.01} = 10.20\%$$

Appendix 3

Full Description of the Attributes

Attribute Assigned Number	Attribute Description
1.	Promptness (Speed) of service.
2.	Professionalism of staff (staff exhibit a thorough knowledge of all available products and services and display skill in helping customers make their choices. Professionally qualified.
3.	Accuracy of information about transactions with the bank.
4.	Clarity of account statements with respect to charges, fees, etc.
5.	Courtesy of staff – smile while getting things done.
6.	Knowledge of staff (generally well educated, have first degree).
7.	Reputation of bank (send out account statement promptly, helps customers solve problems).
8.	Friendliness of staff (call customers by name).
9.	Availability of information about all available services & products.
10.	Convenient hours of operations.
11.	Nice working environment and physical layout.
12.	Availability of equipments to work with.
13.	Generally welcoming, always pleased to go there.
14.	Say thank you.

Reference

Prologue

1. Ambachtsheer K. P. (April 1994): Investment Policy for North American Pension Plans: Investment Policy, AIMR Seminar Proceedings, Tokyo, pp 42-43.

2. Berry et. al. (1985): A Conceptual Model of Service Quality and its Implications for Future Research, Journal of Marketing, Fall 1985, pp4, (In Kotler P (1988) Marketing Management: Analysis, Planning, Implementation, and Control, 6th ed., Prentice Hall of India Private Ltd., New Delhi, pp 484 – 485).

3. Marcus Buckingham (2005): The One Thing You Need to Know: . . . About Great Managing, Great Leading, and Sustained Individual Success: The Audio CD.

4. Peters T. (2010): Tom Peters Daily Quotes in http://www.tompeters.com (tompeters@mail85subscribermail.com)

Chapter One

1. Llewellyn D. (Jan. 1995): The Changing Nature of Banking: Banking World, London, pp 17.

2. Ibid pp 17.

3. Ibid pp 17.

4. Ambachtsheer K. P. (April 1994): Investment Policy for North American Pension Plans: Investment Policy, AIMR Seminar Proceedings, Tokyo, pp 42-43.

5. Gavaghan K. (March 1990): Banks Go Marketing: Banking World, London, pp 17.

6. Pitman B. (April 1988): Banking World, pp 27.

7. Paul U. (1992): Towards Improved Banking Services, The Democrat, March 26, pp 15.

8. Ibid

Chapter Two

1. Stebbing L. (1989): Quality Assurance, the Route to Efficiency and Competitiveness, Ellis Horwood Ltd., UK., pp 1.

2. Juran J. M. (1951): Quality Control Handbook, New York, New York: McGraw-Hill (As Summarised in Soundview Executive Book Summaries, pp 2.)

3. Crosby P. B. (1980): Quality is Free, Signet Books

4. Robson M. (1992): Journey to Excellence (The Video Film)

5. Badiru A. B. and Ayeni B. J. (1993): Practitioner's Guide to Quality and Process Improvement, 1st Edition, Chapman and Hall, London, pp 2.

6. Ibid, pp 2.

7. Ibid, pp 2.

8. Ishikawa K.: Quality Control in Japan (In The Japanese Approach to Quality, It's Applicability to the West: Seminar Proceedings, Sasaki N. and Hutchins D. (Ed.), London, pp 4.

9. Bendell T. (1992): The Quality Gurus: What Can They Do For Your Company? DTI Managing in the 1990s, London, pp 15.

10. Fortuna R. M. (1992): The Quality Imperative (In Total Quality: The Manager's Guide for the 1990s), Huge E. C. (ed.), Kogan Page, London, pp 4.

11. Buzzell R. D. and Gale B. T. (1987): The PIMS Principles: Linking Strategy to Performance, the Free Press, New York, pp 103.

12. Bendell T. (1992): The Quality Gurus: What Can They Do For Your Company? DTI Managing in the 1990s, London, pp 14.

13. Badiru A. B. and Ayeni B. J. (1993): Practitioner's Guide to Quality and Process Improvement, 1st Edition, Chapman and Hall, London, pp 2.

14. Liswood L. A. (1991): Serving Them Right, Harper Business, New York, pp xxiv.

15. Macdonald J. (1993): Understanding Total Quality Management In A Week, British Institute of Management, London, pp 4.

16. Badiru A. B. and Ayeni B. J. (1993): Practitioner's Guide to Quality and Process Improvement, 1st Edition, Chapman and Hall, London, pp 8.

17. Ibid pp 8.

18. Ishikawa K.: Quality Control in Japan (In The Japanese Approach to Quality, It's Applicability to the West: Seminar Proceedings, Sasaki N. and Hutchins D. (Ed.), London, pp 4.

19. Badiru A. B. and Ayeni B. J. (1993): Practitioner's Guide to Quality and Process Improvement, 1st Edition, Chapman and Hall, London, pp 8.

20. Ibid, pp 8 – 9

21. Ibid, 10 – 11.

22. Bendell T. (1992): The Quality Gurus: What Can They Do For Your Company? DTI Managing in the 1990s, London, pp 17.

23. Badiru A. B. and Ayeni B. J. (1993): Practitioner's Guide to Quality and Process Improvement, 1st Edition, Chapman and Hall, London, pp 12.

24. Fortuna R. M. (1992): The Quality Imperative (In Total Quality: The Manager's Guide for the 1990s), Huge E. C. (ed.), Kogan Page, London, pp 25.

25. Badiru A. B. and Ayeni B. J. (1993): Practitioner's Guide to Quality and Process Improvement, 1st Edition, Chapman and Hall, London, pp 15.

26. Ibid, pp 16.

27. The Total Quality Review, Sept./Oct. 1994.

28. Bendell T. (1992): The Quality Gurus: What Can They Do For Your Company? DTI Managing in the 1990s, London, pp 13.

29. Ibid, 17.

30. Badiru A. B. and Ayeni B. J. (1993): Practitioner's Guide to Quality and Process Improvement, 1st Edition, Chapman and Hall, London, pp 17.

31. Bendell T. (1992): The Quality Gurus: What Can They Do For Your Company? DTI Managing in the 1990s, London, pp 4.

32. Bendell T. (1992): The Quality Gurus: What Can They Do For Your Company? DTI Managing in the 1990s, London, pp 4-34.

33. Ibid 35

34. Fortuna R. M. (1992): The Quality Imperative (In Total Quality: The Manager's Guide for the 1990s), Huge E. C. (Ed.), Kogan Page, London, pp 11.

35. Davidow W. H. and Uttal B (1989): Total Customer Service: The Ultimate Weapon, Harper Perennial

36. Crosby P. B. (1988): The Eternally Successful Organisation, McGraw Hill Book Company, pp x.

37. Fortune International, February 8, 1993, pp 21.

38. Stebbing L. (1989): Quality Assurance, the Route to Efficiency and Competitiveness, Ellis Horwood Ltd., UK., pp 3.

39. Liswood L. A. (1991): Serving Them Right, Harper Business, New York, pp 27—47.

40. Macdonald J. (1993): Understanding Total Quality Management In A Week, British Institute of Management, London, pp 16.

41. Liswood L. A. (1991): Serving Them Right, Harper Business, New York, pp 43.

42. Badiru A. B. and Ayeni B. J. (1993): Practitioner's Guide to Quality and Process Improvement, 1ˢᵗ Edition, Chapman and Hall, London, pp 38.

Chapter Three

1. Peters T. J. and Waterman (Jr.) R. H. (1982): In Search of Excellence: Lessons From America's Best-Run Companies, Harper & Row.

2. Macdonald J. (1993): Understanding Total Quality Management In A Week, British Institute of Management, London, pp 4.

3. Badiru A. B. and Ayeni B. J. (1993): Practitioner's Guide to Quality and Process Improvement, 1ˢᵗ Edition, Chapman and Hall, London, pp 29.

4. AIMR (Association of Investment Management and Research, Charlottesville (1993): Seminar Proceedings.

5. Fortuna R. M. (1992): The Quality Imperative (In Total Quality: The Manager's Guide for the 1990s), Huge E. C. (Ed.), Kogan Page, London, pp 3.

6. Robson M. (1992): Journey to Excellence (The Video Film)

7. Badiru A. B. and Ayeni B. J. (1993): Practitioner's Guide to Quality and Process Improvement, 1ˢᵗ Edition, Chapman and Hall, London, pp 38.

8. Walker D. (1990): Customer First: The British Airways Story, pp 103.

9. Ibid, pp 103.

10. Ibid, pp 103.

11. Buzzell R. D. and Gale B. T. (1987): The PIMS Principles: Linking Strategy to Performance, the Free Press, New York, pp 103-134.

12. Ibid, 103 – 134.

13. Ibid, 103 – 104.

14. Ibid, 103 – 104.

15. Ibid, 103 – 104.

16. Fortuna R. M. (1992): The Quality Imperative (In Total Quality: The Manager's Guide for the 1990s), Huge E. C. (Ed.), Kogan Page, London, pp 6.

17. Manchester Business School (1994): Seminar Material. See also Fortuna R. M. (1992): The Quality Imperative, pp 6, and Liswood L. A. (1991): Serving Them Right, pp 7).

18. Liswood L. A. (1991): Serving Them Right, Harper Business, New York, pp 93.

19. Fortuna R. M. (1992): The Quality Imperative (In Total Quality: The Manager's Guide for the 1990s), Huge E. C. (Ed.), Kogan Page, London, pp 11.

20. Manchester Business School (1994): Seminar Material.

21. Ibid

22. Ibid

23. Mckibben S. Ph.D (1990): In Search of Quality: Quality Through People, Action Guide, Vol. 1, Sam Tyler et. al., pp 9.

24. Bendell T. (1992): The Quality Gurus: What Can They Do For Your Company? DTI Managing in the 1990s, London, pp 27.

Chapter Four

1. Kotler P. (1988): Marketing Management: Analysis, Planning, Implementation, and Control, 6th. Ed., Prentice Hall of India Private Ltd., New Delhi, pp 477.

2. Badiru A. B. and Ayeni B. J. (1993): Practitioner's Guide to Quality and Process Improvement, 1st Edition, Chapman and Hall, London, pp 45.

3. Liswood L. A. (1991): Serving Them Right, Harper Business, New York, pp 15-16.

4. Berry et. al. (1985): A Conceptual Model of Service Quality and its Implications for Future Research, Journal of Marketing, Fall 1985, pp 4, (In Kotler P (1988) Marketing Management: Analysis, Planning, Implementation, and Control, 6th ed., Prentice Hall of India Private Ltd., New Delhi, pp 485 – 486).

5. Liswood L. A. (1991): Serving Them Right, Harper Business, New York, pp 92—93.

6. Kotler P. (1988): Marketing Management: Analysis, Planning, Implementation, and Control, 6th. Ed., Prentice Hall of India Private Ltd., New Delhi, pp 486.

7. Berry et. al. (1985): A Conceptual Model of Service Quality and its Implications for Future Research, Journal of Marketing, Fall 1985, pp 4, (In Kotler P (1988) Marketing Management: Analysis, Planning, Implementation, and Control, 6th ed., Prentice Hall of India Private Ltd., New Delhi, pp 484 – 485).

8. Ibid, pp 485.

9. Liswood L. A. (1991): Serving Them Right, Harper Business, New York, pp xxxiv.

10. Sewell C. and Brown P. B. (1992): The Golden Rules of Customer Care, Century Business, London, pp 24.

11. Ibid, pp 24.

12. Ibid, pp 24.

13. Ibid, pp 24.

14. Ansell T (1993): Approaches to Quality Management: Putting it Into Practice at a Local Level: In Financial Services: The Search For Quality, CIB Seminar Proceedings, London, pp 2 – 3.

15. Liswood L. A. (1991): Serving Them Right, Harper Business, New York, pp 110.

16. Ibid, pp 110.

17. Ibid, pp 110.

18. Ibid, pp 110.

19. Ellwood P. (1993): Implementing Total Quality at TSB: In Financial Services: The Search For Quality, CIB Seminar Proceedings, London, pp 91—92.

20. Ibid, pp 92 – 93.

21. Ibid, pp 92 – 93.

22. Ibid, pp 92 – 93.

23. Ibid, pp 92 – 93.

24. Liswood L. A. (1991): Serving Them Right, Harper Business, New York, pp 107—108.

25. Ibid, pp 107 – 108.

26. Ibid, pp 107 – 108.

27. Ibid, pp 107 – 108.

28. Ibid, pp 107 – 108.

29. Ibid, pp 107 – 108.

30. Ibid, pp 107 – 108.

31. Crawley F. (1993): Total Quality Management: A Customer Focused Strategy For Business Improvement. (In *Financial Services: The Search For Quality*, CIB Seminar Proceedings, London, pp 62.

Chapter Five

1. Bennis W. (1998): Organizing Genius: The Secrets of Creative Collaboration, Perseus Books.

2. Covey S. (1989) The Seven Habits of Highly Effective People, Simon and Schuster, New York, pp 101 – 103.

3. Ibid, pp 251

4. Ibid, pp 251

5. Ibid, pp 103, 221.

6. Wallace Company, Inc. (1990): MBNQA Winner: A Condensed Version of the Company's Application for the Award, pp 2.

7. Mckibben S. Ph.D. (1990): In Search of Quality: Quality Through People, Action Guide, Vol. 1, Sam Tyler et. al., pp 13.

Chapter Six

1. Martilla J.A. and John C. J. (1977), "Importance – Performance Analysis", Journal of Marketing, 1977, pp 77 – 79. (In Philip K. (1988): Marketing Management, 6th Ed., pp 487.)

2. Martin W. B. (1989): Managing Quality Customer Service, Kogan Page, pp 81.

3. Liswood L. A. (1991): Serving Them Right, Harper Business, New York, pp 92—93.

4. Berry et. al. (1985): A Conceptual Model of Service Quality and its Implications for Future Research, Journal of Marketing, Fall 1985, pp 4, (In Kotler P (1988) Marketing Management: Analysis, Planning, Implementation, and Control, 6th ed., Prentice Hall of India Private Ltd., New Delhi, pp 486).

5. Adekanye F. (1986): The Elements of Banking in Nigeria, 3rd ed., F & A Publishers Ltd., Lagos, pp 167-169.

6. Nigerian Banking, Finance and Commerce (Research and Data Services Ltd.), (REDASEL), (1985), pp 73.

7. First Bank of Nigeria Plc. Annual Report & Accounts 1993, 1994, 1995.

8. Union Bank of Nigeria Plc. Annual Report & Accounts 1993, 1994, 1995.

9. United Bank for Africa Plc. Annual Report & Accounts 1993, 1994, 1995. http://www.ubagroup.com (last visited on May 28, 2011) http:// www.firstbanknigeria.com (last visited on May 28, 2011) http://www. unionbankng.com (last visited on May 28, 2011)

Chapter Seven

1. Welch J. (with Suzy Welch) (2005): Winning, HarperCollins Publishers.

2. Ibid

3. Ibid

4. Drucker P: In Thomas Strickland (1987): Strategic Management Concepts & Cases, 4th ed., Business Publications Inc., Texas, pp 27.

Epiloque

1. Marcus Buckingham (2005): The One Thing You Need to Know: . . . About Great Managing, Great Leading, and Sustained Individual Success: The Audio CD.